AMERICA'S NATIONAL PARKS

CAPE HATTERAS
NATIONAL SEASHORE

ADVENTURE, EXPLORE, DISCOVER

JENNIFER REED

MyReportLinks.com Books
an imprint of

  Enslow Publishers, Inc.
Box 398, 40 Industrial Road
Berkeley Heights, NJ 07922
USA

MyReportLinks.com Books, an imprint of Enslow Publishers, Inc. MyReportLinks®
is a registered trademark of Enslow Publishers, Inc.

Library of Congress Cataloging-in-Publication Data

Reed, Jennifer, 1967–
  Cape Hatteras National Seashore : adventure, explore, discover / Jennifer Bond Reed.
    p. cm. — (America's national parks)
  Includes bibliographical references and index.
  ISBN-13: 978-1-59845-086-6 (hardcover)
  ISBN-10: 1-59845-086-7 (hardcover)
  1. Cape Hatteras National Seashore (N.C.)—History—Juvenile literature. 2. Cape Hatteras
National Seashore (N.C.)—Description and travel—Juvenile literature. I. Title.
F262.O96R44 2008
975.6'175—dc22
                                    2006102321

Printed in the United States of America

10 9 8 7 6 5 4 3 2 1

To Our Readers:
Through the purchase of this book, you and your library gain access to the Report Links that specifically back up this book.
The Publisher will provide access to the Report Links that back up this book and will keep these Report Links up to date on **www.myreportlinks.com** for five years from the book's first publication date.
We have done our best to make sure all Internet addresses in this book were active and appropriate when we went to press. However, the author and the Publisher have no control over, and assume no liability for, the material available on those Internet sites or on other Web sites they may link to.
The usage of the MyReportLinks.com Books Web site is subject to the terms and conditions stated on the Usage Policy Statement on **www.myreportlinks.com**.
A password may be required to access the Report Links that back up this book. The password is found on the bottom of page 4 of this book.
Any comments or suggestions can be sent by e-mail to comments@myreportlinks.com or to the address on the back cover.

C‹ Enslow Publishers, Inc., is committed to printing our books on recycled paper. The paper in every book contains 10% to 30% post-consumer waste (PCW). The cover board on the outside of each book contains 100% PCW. Our goal is to do our part to help young people and the environment too!

Photo Credits: accessgenealogy.com, p. 24; © AP/Wide World Photos (Bob Jordan), pp. 62–63, 88 (*Richmond Times-Dispatch,* Don Long); blackbeardscastle.com, p. 12; Civilian Conservation Corps, p. 42; DesertUSA.com, p. 74; Enslow Publishers, Inc., p. 17; Fish & Wildlife Service, p. 6 (plover) & 77, 78; Frisco Native American Museum and Natural History Center, p. 26; GORP.com, p. 102; The Granger Collection, p. 32; Graveyard of the Atlantic Museum, p. 47; Institute of Nautical Archaeology, p. 38; istockphoto.com, pp. 6 (Ocracoke Beach) & 7 (seagull at sunset), 18–19, 66, 112; Library of Congress, p. 52; The Mariners' Museum, p. 53; MyReportLinks.com Books, p. 4; National Oceanic and Atmospheric Association (NOAA), pp. 29, 58, 75, 90, 92; National Park Service, pp. 5 (map), 21, 30, 40 (Chris Wonderly), 56, 72; National Parks Conservation Association, p. 93; National Parks Foundation, p. 109; National Underwater and Marine Agency, p. 50; National Weather Service, pp. 86, 103; North Carolina Coastal Reserve Program, p. 94; North Carolina Department of Commerce, Division of Tourism, p. 101; North Carolina Maritime Museum, p. 10; North Carolina Wildlife Resources Commission, p. 68; Outer Banks Visitors Bureau, p. 14; PBS, p. 59; Photos.com, pp. 1 (photo of Cape Hatteras lighthouse), 6 (Bodie Light), 8–9 (Blackbeard), 25, 106–107; Roanoke Island Festival Park, p. 116; Shutterstock.com, pp. 1(background photo of dune), 3, 7 (hang gliding at Jockey's Ridge and loggerhead turtle), 16 (Jill Lang), 18–19 (laptop), 40 (cell phone), 44, 66–67 (Palm Pilot), 80–81, 84–85 (beach & computer), 96, 98–99 (horses and camera), 114–115 (Lyn Adams); Smithsonian Museum of Natural History, p. 20; State Library of North Carolina, pp. 28, 34; University of Wisconsin, p. 37.

Cover Photo: Photos.com

CONTENTS

MyReportLinks.com Books
Great Books, Great Links, Great for Research!

The Internet sites featured in this book can save you hours of research time. These Internet sites—we call them **"Report Links"**—are constantly changing, but we keep them up to date on our Web site.

When you see this "Approved Web Site" logo, you will know that we are directing you to a great Internet site that will help you with your research.

Give it a try! Type http://www.myreportlinks.com into your browser, click on the series title and enter the password, then click on the book title, and scroll down to the Report Links listed for this book.

The Report Links will bring you to great source documents, photographs, and illustrations. MyReportLinks.com Books save you time, feature Report Links that are kept up to date, and make report writing easier than ever! A complete listing of the Report Links can be found on pages 118–119 at the back of the book.

Please see "To Our Readers" on the copyright page for important information about this book, the MyReportLinks.com Web site, and the Report Links that back up this book.

Please enter **CNP1865** if asked for a password.

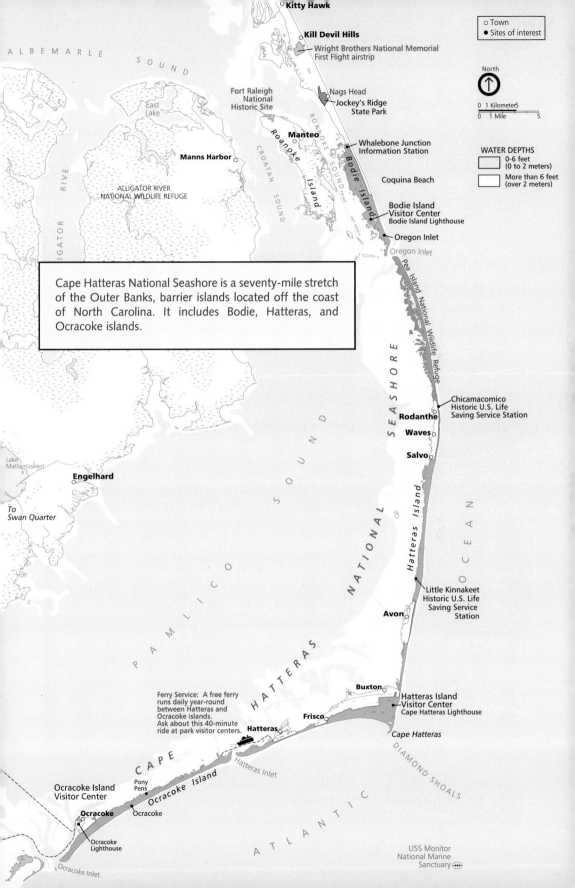

Kitty Hawk

○ Town
● Sites of interest

Kill Devil Hills
Wright Brothers National Memorial
First Flight airstrip

North

0   1 Kilometer 5
0   1 Mile   5

ALBEMARLE SOUND

East Lake

Fort Raleigh National Historic Site

Nags Head
Jockey's Ridge State Park

Manteo

Roanoke Island

Manns Harbor

Whalebone Junction Information Station

Croatan Sound

Coquina Beach

ALLIGATOR RIVER NATIONAL WILDLIFE REFUGE

ALLIGATOR RIVE

Bodie Island

WATER DEPTHS
0-6 feet (0 to 2 meters)
More than 6 feet (over 2 meters)

Bodie Island Visitor Center
Bodie Island Lighthouse

Oregon Inlet

Oregon Inlet

Cape Hatteras National Seashore is a seventy-mile stretch of the Outer Banks, barrier islands located off the coast of North Carolina. It includes Bodie, Hatteras, and Ocracoke islands.

Pea Island National Wildlife Refuge

SEASHORE

Chicamacomico Historic U.S. Life Saving Service Station

Rodanthe
Waves

Lake Mattamuskeet

Engelhard

Salvo

PAMLICO SOUND

Hatteras Island

To Swan Quarter

NATIONAL

OCEAN

Little Kinnakeet Historic U.S. Life Saving Service Station

Avon

HATTERAS

Ferry Service: A free ferry runs daily year-round between Hatteras and Ocracoke islands. Ask about this 40-minute ride at park visitor centers.

Buxton

Hatteras Island Visitor Center
Cape Hatteras Lighthouse

Frisco

Hatteras

Cape Hatteras

CAPE

Hatteras Inlet

DIAMOND SHOALS

Ocracoke Island Visitor Center

Pony Pens

Ocracoke Island

Ocracoke

Ocracoke

ATLANTIC

Ocracoke Lighthouse

USS Monitor National Marine Sanctuary

Ocracoke Inlet

CAPE HATTERAS

🐚 Cape Hatteras National Seashore is one of the most visited national parks in the United States. It was the first national seashore in America.

⭐ Cape Hatteras National Seashore is part of the Atlantic Flyway, a bird migration route that stretches from the Canadian Maritimes to the Gulf of Mexico. Many birds pass through the Outer Banks during migration.

🐚 Wildlife is plentiful here, including birds, fish, crabs, and other creatures.

⭐ Cape Hatteras National Seashore is 70 miles (113 km) long.

🐚 Cape Hatteras Light is the tallest brick lighthouse in North America. It was moved a distance of 2,900 feet (884 meters) in 1999.

⭐ Hundreds of shipwrecks have occurred off the coast of Cape Hatteras.

🐚 Pirates frequently visited the Outer Banks, including Cape Hatteras. Blackbeard the pirate lived, pirated, and died on the Outer Banks.

⭐ Early American Indian tribes on the Outer Banks were called Croatans, and later became known as Hatteras.

🐚 Wild Spanish mustangs roamed freely on the Outer Banks until 1959.

⭐ Cape Hatteras National Seashore and the Outer Banks are always moving. They are barrier islands made up of sand and sandbars.

NATIONAL SEASHORE FACTS

- Many of the seashells found on the beach are thousands of years old.

- Biking, kayaking, boating, swimming, golfing, and fishing are just some of the activities enjoyed by vacationers at Cape Hatteras National Seashore.

- Concrete seawalls cannot be built along Cape Hatteras National Seashore.

- Sand dunes on Cape Hatteras National Seashore are always changing.

- Buxton Woods on Hatteras Island is the largest maritime forest in North Carolina.

- Sometimes the crabs glow in the dark!

- Trees located here cannot grow very tall because a salty wind is constantly blowing.

- Manatees and sea lions have been known to visit the waters off Cape Hatteras.

- German U-boats were often sighted during World War II off the coast of Cape Hatteras National Seashore.

- Hurricane Hazel (in 1954) was one of the worst hurricanes to hit this area. Its winds were at 150 mph when it reached land.

- Cape Hatteras National Seashore is one of the best bird-watching sites on the Atlantic Coast.

- Sea turtles such as the endangered logger-head make their nests on the beach at Cape Hatteras. Only one in a thousand sea turtles survive to adulthood.

Chapter

This 1734 engraving by Thomas Nicholls shows Blackbeard, a notorious pirate of the early eighteenth century. He used to strike fear into the hearts of sailors by lighting small wicks tied in his beard on fire.

Shiver Me Timbers!

Edward Teach was thought to be a native of Bristol, England. Teach turned to pirating in the early 1700s. He became known as Blackbeard and was feared by all.

Blackbeard boarded the French slave ship *Concorde*. He stared at the crew with a devilish grin. *Concorde*'s crew trembled. Standing tall, Blackbeard hovered over most people. He had the blackest beard, which seemed to cover his entire face. Bows were tied throughout his beard. Each bow had a wick in it. Blackbeard lit the wicks so smoke rose all around his face, making him look like a monster to many sailors.

He wore a red coat, and carried two swords at his waist. He had numerous guns and knives. The sight of Blackbeard was enough to make any sailor cry, "Shiver me timbers!"

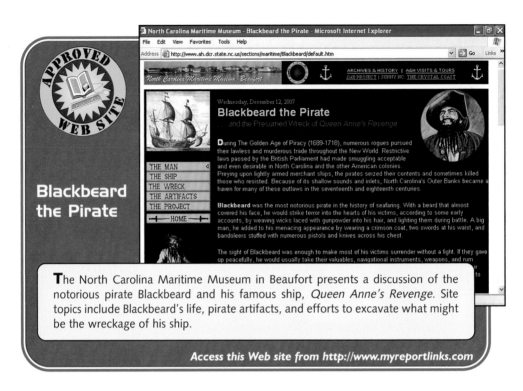

The North Carolina Maritime Museum in Beaufort presents a discussion of the notorious pirate Blackbeard and his famous ship, *Queen Anne's Revenge*. Site topics include Blackbeard's life, pirate artifacts, and efforts to excavate what might be the wreckage of his ship.

Access this Web site from http://www.myreportlinks.com

As Blackbeard is described in the 1724 work, *A General History of the Robberies and Murders of the most notorious Pyrates*:

> In time of action, he wore a sling over his shoulders, with three brace of pistols, hanging in holsters like bandoliers; he wore a fur-cap, and stuck a lighted match on each side, under it, which appearing on each side his face, his eyes naturally looking fierce and wild, made him altogether such a figure, that imagination cannot form an idea of a fury, from Hell, to look more frightful.[1]

It was easy work for Blackbeard to steal the *Concorde*. It happened off the coast of St. Vincent in the Caribbean in November 1717. The *Concorde* became Blackbeard's flagship. He renamed it

Queen Anne's Revenge. A short while later, he teamed up with another pirate, Stede Bonnet. During the winter of 1717–1718, the two pirates raided ships and made off with their cargo.

In May 1718, Blackbeard sailed *Queen Anne's Revenge* up to Charleston, South Carolina. Four of his ships blocked the entrance to the port. Four hundred pirates raided and stole the cargo of ships coming and going from the port. It was one of Blackbeard's most successful moments as a pirate.

Blackbeard, along with his crew and ships, was wanted by the government of Great Britain. He stayed at Ocracoke Inlet, North Carolina. He wanted to fortify this area with pirates, but it would not happen. The British ship HMS *Pearl* captained by Lieutenant Robert Maynard sat off the coast of Ocracoke waiting for Blackbeard.

Blackbeard, aboard another of his ships named *Adventure,* thought it would be easy to take over Maynard and his crew. There was a short battle between the ships. Maynard blew up *Adventure*'s rigging, forcing it ashore.

Maynard cleared the decks of his crew to trick Blackbeard so he thought it was safe to board the *Pearl.* When he did, Maynard's men emerged and a battle broke out. Blackbeard was killed. His head was cut off and used as a trophy on Maynard's ship. Blackbeard's body was flung overboard.

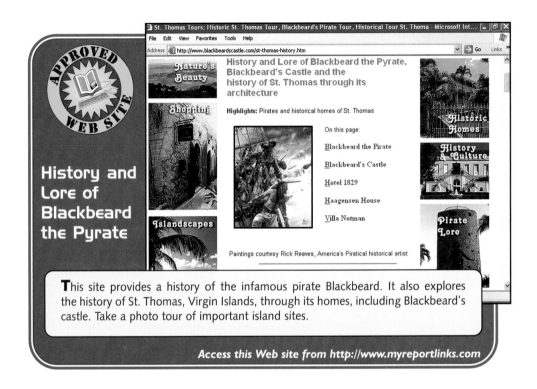

History and Lore of Blackbeard the Pyrate

St. Thomas Tours: Historic St. Thomas Tour, Blackbeard's Pirate Tour, Historical Tour St. Thoma - Microsoft Int...

File   Edit   View   Favorites   Tools   Help

Address http://www.blackbeardscastle.com/st-thomas-history.htm   Go   Links

Nature's Beauty

Shopping

Islandscapes

History and Lore of Blackbeard the Pyrate, Blackbeard's Castle and the history of St. Thomas through its architecture

Highlights: Pirates and historical homes of St. Thomas

On this page:

Blackbeard the Pirate

Blackbeard's Castle

Hotel 1829

Haagensen House

Villa Notman

Paintings courtesy Rick Reeves, America's Piratical historical artist

Historic Homes

History & Culture

Pirate Lore

This site provides a history of the infamous pirate Blackbeard. It also explores the history of St. Thomas, Virgin Islands, through its homes, including Blackbeard's castle. Take a photo tour of important island sites.

Access this Web site from http://www.myreportlinks.com

Some said that his headless body swam around his ship seven times. The golden age of piracy had ended.

In 1997, scientists found the sunken *Queen Anne's Revenge*. More than two thousand artifacts have been located. Blackbeard took valuable items from other ships. Not all the treasures were gold and silver; some of the items included scientific instruments and medical supplies.

Pirate ships were armed with many weapons. Eighteen cannons were located, along with some of Blackbeard's personal items. These included a pipe, buttons, bottles, and gold dust. Today, many people travel to the Outer Banks and Cape

Hatteras National Seashore, North Carolina, just to see if they can find treasures from sunken ships. Sometimes they do!

CAPE HATTERAS NATIONAL SEASHORE

Tales of treasure, ships, and pirates of the Outer Banks, North Carolina are popular with local residents and visitors. This area of the United States is filled with history. To preserve it and the wildlife here, Cape Hatteras National Seashore was developed. It is a stretch of beach seventy miles long. This beach includes marshes, maritime forests, historical sites, and landmarks.

It stretches south across three islands—Bodie, Hatteras, and Ocracoke. The islands are connected by Highway 12 and the Hatteras Inlet Ferry. Ocracoke's name is believed to be Indian in origin. Early maps show the island's name as "Woccocon," and by 1715 the name had become "Ococcock." Soon after, the name began to appear on maps as "Ocracoke."[2]

In the early 1900s, it became clear to the local residents and visitors that this area was a national resource and must be protected. Because of the landscape, the Outer Banks were open to the wind and sea. The sand was constantly moving and changing. Storms ravaged the seashore and often destroyed what was there. All it would take was one major storm to destroy it all. In order to make

The Outer Banks of North Carolina® Visitors Bureau - Microsoft Internet Explorer

File   Edit   View   Favorites   Tools   Help

Address http://www.outerbanks.org/   Go   Links »

HOME | DIRECTORY | WHERE TO PLAY | WHERE TO STAY | WHERE TO EAT | GUIDE | CALENDAR | GETTING HERE | FAQS

The Outer Banks®
OF NORTH CAROLINA

Clickable Map

Duck
Southern Shores
Kitty Hawk
Kill Devil Hills
Nags Head

A Delicate Chain of
Barrier Islands
Welcome to the Outer Banks of North Carolina.
Since 1587, people have been drawn to our
undisturbed beauty. More than 420 years later,
visitors still marvel at the quiet sanctuary that
lies before them as the historical imprints our
many visitors have left behind. The Outer
Banks of North Carolina mixes the past and
the present into a well-kept balance of solitude
and activity that is ideal for all ages and
spirits.

It's easy to find us along the North Carolina

Learn much more about the history, museums, and wildlife found on
The Outer Banks of North Carolina. The Visitors Bureau's site includes
a section on lighthouses, an interactive map, and list of upcoming events in
the area.

EDITOR'S CHOICE

it a protected area, Cape Hatteras National Seashore had to be established as an ecologically valuable and fragile area.

In the 1930s, President Franklin Roosevelt created a public works program called the Civilian Conservation Corps (CCC). One of the CCC's many efforts to save the nation's natural resources was to build a line of sand dunes to act as a barrier at Cape Hatteras National Seashore, thus protecting the area from wind and waves.

The dunes are not a permanent solution, but they have worked for nearly eighty years. Storms wash out roads and sometimes bury areas with five or six feet of sand. Cape Hatteras National Seashore and the Outer Banks have not changed that much over the years. But all it takes is one strong hurricane to transform the landscape completely.

⇒ RESIDENTS AND VISITORS

Cape Hatteras National Seashore is a popular place to visit. The peak season is summer. The water is warm, around 70°F (21°C). Light breezes keep it comfortable, and there is a lot to see and do. A United States Census Bureau estimate from 2006 indicated that about sixty-three thousand people permanently live on the Outer Banks, and more than one million people visit each year. Because there are so many people flocking to the seashore, it's become more important than ever to preserve the area.

Cape Hatteras National Seashore does not include the villages that were built nearby. While towns like Salvo, Buxton, Rodanthe, and Hatteras are not part of the national seashore, they provide services to the people who live and visit the area. Stores and restaurants give shoppers plenty to do on rainy days. Museums and places of historical importance are also found in the towns.

The most popular places to visit, in addition to the beach, are the lighthouses. Cape Hatteras

At a height of 208 feet, the Cape Hatteras lighthouse is the tallest brick lighthouse in the United States. Its distinctive black and white spiral stripes serve as its unique daymark, or daytime identification.

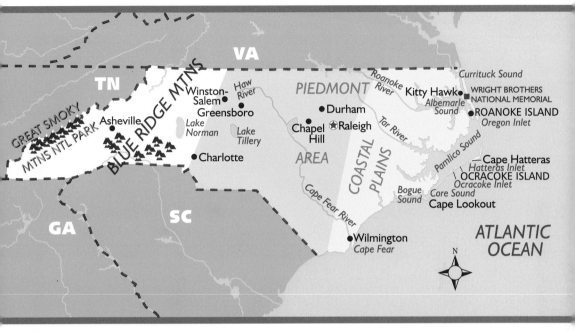

▲ *This map shows the location of Cape Hatteras National Seashore in relation to the rest of North Carolina.*

National Seashore has three lighthouses: Bodie Light, Cape Hatteras Light, and Ocracoke Light. Perhaps the most famous and well known is Cape Hatteras Light. All three lighthouses served a vital purpose during America's great shipping era. The waters off the coast of the Outer Banks were not a safe place to sail. There are estimated to be more than one thousand shipwrecks in these waters. For this reason, it is known as the Graveyard of the Atlantic.

With so much to see and do, Cape Hatteras National Seashore is one of the most popular vacation destinations in the United States.

Chapter 2

Ocracoke Beach is just one of the attractions of Cape Hatteras National Seashore.

The Ever-Changing Seashore

The long stretch of barrier islands just off the North Carolina coast is called the Outer Banks. Part of this stretch of sand has been designated the Cape Hatteras National Seashore. It took a long time to form these islands. They started forming around the time of the Ice Age. Since then, the islands of the Outer Banks have been constantly changing and moving.

Forests once covered the islands. American Indians lived and thrived there, and food was plentiful. Today, the islands are mostly sand. Only a few trees remain from long ago. There is a maritime forest, but it is small compared to the forests that once covered the area.

Geologists believe that the Outer Banks were formed about ten thousand years ago. Their formation was influenced by

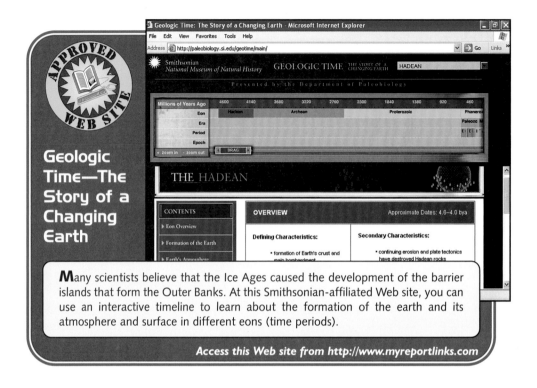

Geologic Time—The Story of a Changing Earth

Many scientists believe that the Ice Ages caused the development of the barrier islands that form the Outer Banks. At this Smithsonian-affiliated Web site, you can use an interactive timeline to learn about the formation of the earth and its atmosphere and surface in different eons (time periods).

Access this Web site from http://www.myreportlinks.com

several factors, including the end of the Ice Age and the motion of wind and waves. Although no one is certain how the Outer Banks were formed, one theory makes a lot of sense.

→THE FORMATION OF THE OUTER BANKS

Before the Ice Age, the North American continent was covered with trees and vegetation. The Outer Banks, it is thought, made up a ridgeline about four hundred feet or more above the level of the ocean. A ridgeline is a group of hills and mountains. These hills and mountains had valleys to the west of them.

After the Ice Age, the terrain underwent an extreme change. Much of the North American continent was covered in ice. The ice was a huge glacier. The Ice Age ended about ten thousand years ago, and glacial melt began to make the sea level rise. The waves and wind continued to pound the ridge to the west. The ocean rose higher until it carved new rivers into the ridge.

Soon there was a great deal of water, and nowhere for it to go. The valleys behind the ridge-line flooded. The ocean overtook the ridge and formed a sound behind it. A sound is a body of

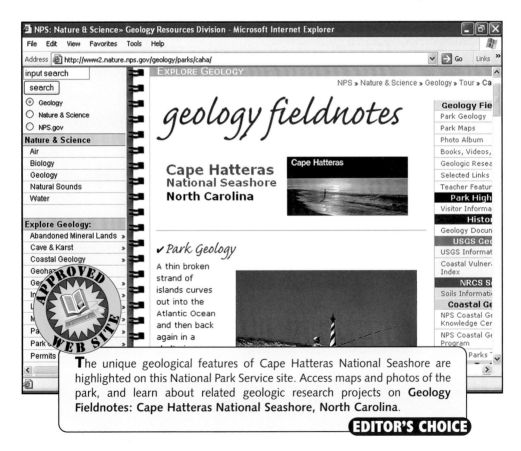

The unique geological features of Cape Hatteras National Seashore are highlighted on this National Park Service site. Access maps and photos of the park, and learn about related geologic research projects on **Geology Fieldnotes: Cape Hatteras National Seashore, North Carolina**.

EDITOR'S CHOICE

water between two landforms. The sound divides the barrier islands from the mainland, and is often calmer than the ocean. The ocean level continued to rise until just a bit of land was left. This land became the barrier islands seen today, the Outer Banks.

Barrier islands are found all along the East Coast. They are most famous along the North Carolina coastline. Three barrier islands make up the Outer Banks. They are Bodie Island, Hatteras Island, and Ocracoke Island.

The barrier islands were once much farther out to sea than they are now. The shoreline was about fifty feet east of its current location.[1] Waves pushed sand onto the ridge. This constant motion continued to build the islands and moved them westward over a period of thousands of years to where they are today.

SEA LEVEL CHANGES

The sea level has generally remained at its current level for the last twelve hundred years. The size and shape of the Outer Banks have not changed much over the years either. However, the sea level is now rising at a rate of about one foot per century.[2] Glaciers are melting all over the world due to global warming. This is causing the water in the ocean to rise. When the sea level rises, islands disappear.

Many people think the barrier islands will continue to move westward. Wind and waves constantly pick up sand and deposit it on beaches. Sand is blown from the east side of the islands to the west. Each time there is a storm like a hurricane, huge amounts of water flow over the islands and into the sound behind them. The water carries sand and sediment. This causes beach erosion.

The Outer Banks are always under attack. The beach is eroded on the east side of the islands, while sand carried by wind and waves is added to the west. Many homes that now sit along the shoreline will someday be underwater.

AMERICAN INDIANS ON THE OUTER BANKS

American Indians have lived on the barrier islands of North Carolina for thousands of years. The Indians were called Algonquian. Algonquian was a related group of languages that many American Indians spoke along the East Coast. The tribes on the Outer Banks were called Croatans and later became known as Hatteras.

Hatteras Island had the only permanent American Indian village, which had been there for about eight hundred years. This island is wider than the other islands, and offered more room to plant crops. The Hatteras used the other islands for fishing and hunting.

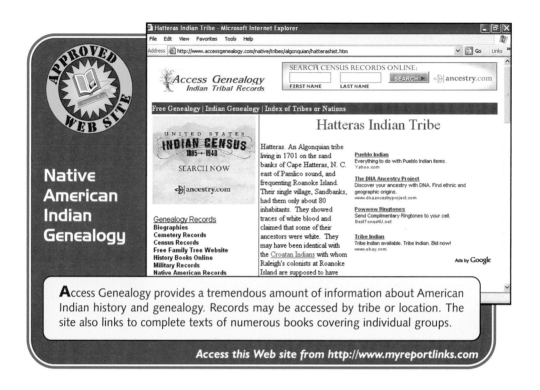

Access Genealogy provides a tremendous amount of information about American Indian history and genealogy. Records may be accessed by tribe or location. The site also links to complete texts of numerous books covering individual groups.

Access this Web site from http://www.myreportlinks.com

Not much is known about these American Indians. They lived before written history was kept. Notes and drawings from early explorers and findings from archaeological digs do provide some information about them.

For the most part, the American Indians here lived peacefully. Because they did not move around with the migration of herds, they were more established. They hunted small game such as fish and birds. Seafood was also a mainstay of their diet. The natives ate clams, scallops, fish, oysters, and mussels. They depended on gardening and knew how to grow crops such as corn, squash, and beans. The Indians made pottery from clay and crushed seashells. They also developed ways to make cloth. Because there were many forests, they built their homes—called longhouses—from wood.

The land and sea were filled with natural resources. The Indians only had to worry about warring neighbor tribes. Still, there was enough land and space for everyone. At least that's the

▲ *The huts and longhouses of an Algonquian Indian village in Pomeiock, near present-day Gibbs Creek, N.C., as drawn by John White in 1585.*

Welcome to Frisco Native American Museum - Microsoft Internet Explorer

File   Edit   View   Favorites   Tools   Help

Address   http://www.nativeamericanmuseum.org/index.htm   Go   Links

Frisco Native American Museum & Natural History Center

Home | Museum | Photos | Gift Shop | Nature Trails | Links | Powwow | Contact

Located on Hatteras Island on the Outer Banks of North Carolina, the Frisco Native American Museum and Natural History Center is a non-profit educational foundation created for the purpose of preserving Native American artifacts, art, and culture.

Location: Hwy 12, Frisco, NC.
[Map & Driving directions]
Hours: 11a.m. - 5 p.m.
Open: Tuesday - Sunday.
(Monday by appointment only)
Winter Hours Adjusted.
Admission:
$5 per person,
$15 per family,
$3 for seniors.
Services: Guided tours and lectures for school and youth groups are available with notic
Facilities: Newly expanded his center and bookstore.
Contact:
P.O. Box 399, Frisco, NC 2793€
Tel: (252) 995-4440
Fax: (252) 995-4030
admin@nativeamericanmuseur

The Frisco Native American Museum and Natural History Center is a nonprofit educational foundation that works to preserve American Indian artifacts, art, and culture. Its site features a photo gallery of the museum's collection of artifacts, and links to Web sites for those interested in American Indian cultures.

way it seemed until the first white explorers showed up.

On March 1, 1524, an Italian explorer named Giovanni da Verrazzano landed near Cape Fear, North Carolina. The American Indians he met were friendly. He wrote to the king of France about what he saw: "The people are of a color russet [reddish brown], and not much unlike the Saracens [Arabs]; their hair black, thick, and not very long, which they tie together in a knot behind, and wear it like a tail."[3]

Soon, more explorers came to the barrier islands. A colony was established at Roanoke Island in 1587. But when the governor of the colony returned from England more than two years later, the colony had vanished. The mystery of what happened to this colony remains, and archaeological and DNA research projects are part of the continuing efforts to find answers.

Colonies were not established for a long time after this, but Europeans continued to come to the barrier islands. With them came diseases such as smallpox, influenza, measles, and typhus, which destroyed 50 to 90 percent of the native population. The natives did not have immunity to the foreign diseases.

Land disputes occurred between the Indians and white explorers. Some Indians were forced into slavery. Wars broke out between other tribes and the explorers. This and the reduced numbers of natives made it difficult for the American Indians of the Outer Banks to survive. Those who were left were sent to special areas of land created just for American Indians. Others lived with the colonists. By about 1750, the once-great society of the Carolina Algonquian had disappeared.

⊜ STRIPPING THE FOREST

The early explorers and settlers of the sixteenth and seventeenth centuries saw the woods on the

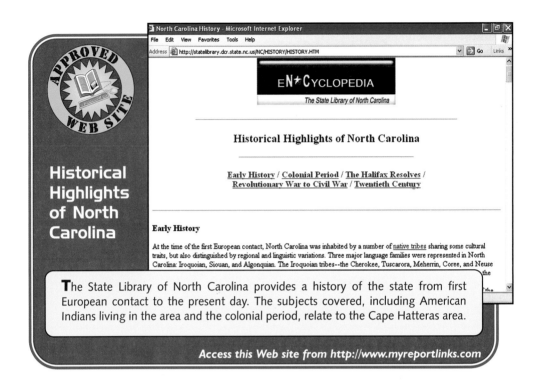

eN✫Cyclopedia

The State Library of North Carolina

Historical Highlights of North Carolina

Early History / Colonial Period / The Halifax Resolves /
Revolutionary War to Civil War / Twentieth Century

Early History

At the time of the first European contact, North Carolina was inhabited by a number of native tribes sharing some cultural traits, but also distinguished by regional and linguistic variations. Three major language families were represented in North Carolina: Iroquoian, Siouan, and Algonquian. The Iroquoian tribes--the Cherokee, Tuscarora, Meherrin, Coree, and Neuse

Historical Highlights of North Carolina

The State Library of North Carolina provides a history of the state from first European contact to the present day. The subjects covered, including American Indians living in the area and the colonial period, relate to the Cape Hatteras area.

Access this Web site from http://www.myreportlinks.com

barrier islands as a great opportunity. They were thick with lumber. Many forests in Europe had been cut down, and wood was hard to obtain. These explorers found a lot of wood and an easy way to ship it home. There were riches to be made, but these people failed to consider the lasting impact of their lumbering on the land.

Because the trees were on the coast, the explorers did not have to haul them far over land. But shipping heavy logs overseas could be a problem because of the wave conditions in the North Atlantic. Fortunately, the Gulf Stream passed near the islands. The Gulf Stream is a warm and powerful current in the Atlantic Ocean. It travels up the coastline to Newfoundland where it meets the North Atlantic Drift and then crosses over to England.[4]

Early explorers made use of the Gulf Stream to export the lumber to England. It was a good business for many early explorers, but it was not good for the Outer Banks. The land was stripped of most of its trees.[5] Much of the vegetation was destroyed, and so were many habitats. Today, only a few trees can be dated back to this time.

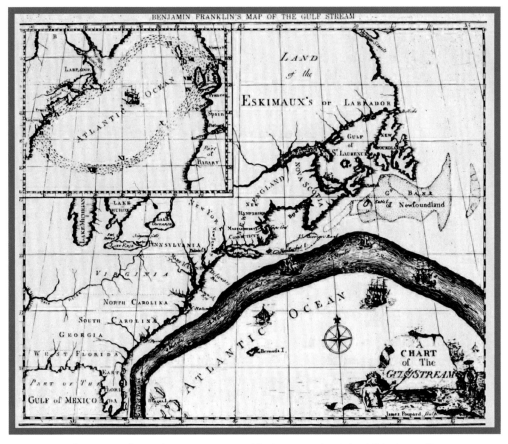

▲ *A map drawn by Benjamin Franklin in approximately 1782 shows the path of the Gulf Stream as it passes near Cape Hatteras.*

In the eighteenth and nineteenth centuries, some forests grew back only to be cut down again. This left the Outer Banks open to the harsh forces of the ocean. Strong winds and salt spray make it difficult for plants to grow here. Since the 1600s, the land of the Outer Banks has changed considerably compared to its appearance and location when the early explorers arrived. Without vegetation to hold the sand in place, the islands continue to move westward.

⊛THE LOST COLONY

Before the colonies of Jamestown, Virginia, and Plymouth, Massachusetts, a small group of people

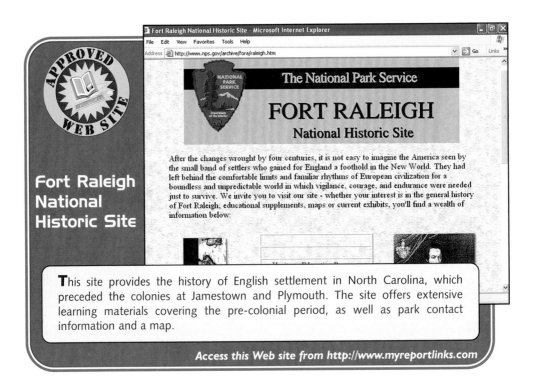

Fort Raleigh National Historic Site

The National Park Service

FORT RALEIGH
National Historic Site

After the changes wrought by four centuries, it is not easy to imagine the America seen by the small band of settlers who gained for England a foothold in the New World. They had left behind the comfortable limits and familiar rhythms of European civilization for a boundless and unpredictable world in which vigilance, courage, and endurance were needed just to survive. We invite you to visit our site - whether your interest is in the general history of Fort Raleigh, educational supplements, maps or current exhibits, you'll find a wealth of information below:

This site provides the history of English settlement in North Carolina, which preceded the colonies at Jamestown and Plymouth. The site offers extensive learning materials covering the pre-colonial period, as well as park contact information and a map.

Access this Web site from http://www.myreportlinks.com

sailed from England to start a new life in the New World. Mystery surrounds these people. Because the records at that time were not good, many questions arise about what is now known as "the Lost Colony."

Some of the earliest explorers included Sir Francis Drake and John White. They had been to the area of the Outer Banks, and felt it would be a good place to start a new colony.

Sir Walter Raleigh chose John White to settle on Roanoke Island, North Carolina. This small island is just to the west of the Outer Banks. In May 1587, three ships set sail for the New World. They left England with 115 settlers. This included seventeen women, two of whom were pregnant, and eleven children. They finally landed in July and established the first colony. Virginia Dare was the first child born in the New World.

MYSTERY OF THE LOST COLONY

John White decided to return to England for more supplies. He felt the colonists were safe and able to survive on their own for awhile. White thought he would return a year later. However, he did not actually return for more than two years. Many people think that the colonists felt White had abandoned them, and that they would have to rely on the natives to survive.

This engraving depicts John White's return to the site of the colony at Roanoke Island, N.C., only to find the word "CROATOAN" carved into a tree. There were no other signs of the "Lost Colony."

When John White finally returned in 1590, there was no trace of the colony. Only the letters CRO carved in a tree, and the word CROATOAN carved in an entrance post, were found.

Many wonder what became of the colonists. Were they attacked by the natives? Did they all die from disease? Did they move somewhere else? These questions remain in the minds of many people who live and visit the area. The most logical explanation is that the settlers were taken in by the natives and lived with them. It would be many years until England seriously pursued colonization in the new world. The next colony to be established was Jamestown, Virginia, in 1607.

Today, visitors can find little evidence that the first settlers of the Lost Colony existed. Geologist Robert Dolan said that the settlers would have built on the highest, most stable part of the island. Hunting and farming would have been done between the fort and the shore. Due to erosion and storms, however, the place where the settlers lived is thought to possibly be under water.[6]

➡ PIRATES AND SHIPWRECKS

The golden age of piracy, which lasted from 1689 to 1718, brought terror to the Outer Banks. This lasted from 1689 to 1718. Blackbeard was one of the most well-known pirates. Gold and silver

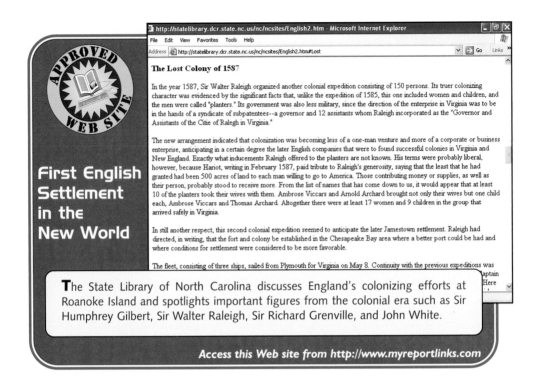

APPROVED WEB SITE

First English
Settlement
in the
New World

http://statelibrary.dcr.state.nc.us/nc/ncsites/English2.htm - Microsoft Internet Explorer

File   Edit   View   Favorites   Tools   Help

Address http://statelibrary.dcr.state.nc.us/nc/ncsites/English2.htm#Lost   Go   Links

The Lost Colony of 1587

In the year 1587, Sir Walter Raleigh organized another colonial expedition consisting of 150 persons. Its truer colonizing character was evidenced by the significant facts that, unlike the expedition of 1585, this one included women and children, and the men were called "planters." Its government was also less military, since the direction of the enterprise in Virginia was to be in the hands of a syndicate of subpatentees--a governor and 12 assistants whom Raleigh incorporated as the "Governor and Assistants of the Citie of Ralegh in Virginia."

The new arrangement indicated that colonization was becoming less of a one-man venture and more of a corporate or business enterprise, anticipating in a certain degree the later English companies that were to found successful colonies in Virginia and New England. Exactly what inducements Raleigh offered to the planters are not known. His terms were probably liberal, however, because Hariot, writing in February 1587, paid tribute to Raleigh's generosity, saying that the least that he had granted had been 500 acres of land to each man willing to go to America. Those contributing money or supplies, as well as their person, probably stood to receive more. From the list of names that has come down to us, it would appear that at least 10 of the planters took their wives with them. Ambrose Viccars and Arnold Archard brought not only their wives but one child each, Ambrose Viccars and Thomas Archard. Altogether there were at least 17 women and 9 children in the group that arrived safely in Virginia.

In still another respect, this second colonial expedition seemed to anticipate the later Jamestown settlement. Raleigh had directed, in writing, that the fort and colony be established in the Chesapeake Bay area where a better port could be had and where conditions for settlement were considered to be more favorable.

The fleet, consisting of three ships, sailed from Plymouth for Virginia on May 8. Continuity with the previous expeditions was

The State Library of North Carolina discusses England's colonizing efforts at Roanoke Island and spotlights important figures from the colonial era such as Sir Humphrey Gilbert, Sir Walter Raleigh, Sir Richard Grenville, and John White.

Access this Web site from http://www.myreportlinks.com

mined in South America and parts of North America were shipped to England and Europe. Often, the ships loaded with treasures were slow and poorly armed. This made them easy targets.

The few small settlements that existed in the Outer Banks were in danger of being attacked. Pirates used these settlements to rest and "make merry" between jobs. The barrier islands were a perfect place to hide and wait for an unsuspecting ship to pass by.

Pirates regularly cruised the waters between the Outer Banks and the Caribbean. They plundered ships and stole the cargo on board. Sometimes they killed the crew. Many pirates and their crews became wealthy, like Blackbeard. The life of a pirate was exciting, but it was also dangerous.

A COLORFUL CAST OF PIRATES

Some other famous pirates who often visited the Outer Banks were Stede Bonnet, Anne Bonny, and Calico Jack Rackham. Calico Jack got his name from the colorful calico clothes he wore. He became famous not just because of his plundering, but because he worked with two famous female pirates, Anne Bonny and Mary Read.[7] Calico Jack and Anne Bonny stole a sloop and found a crew. Calico Jack did not think the crew would work with a woman, so Anne Bonny dressed like a man and called herself Adam Bonny. She soon earned the respect of the crew.

Calico Jack was hung in 1720 for piracy along with much of his crew. Anne Bonny and Mary Read were sent to prison also to be executed. Both women said they were pregnant, so their hangings were delayed until after their babies were born. However, Mary Read died while in prison. Strangely enough, there is no further record of Anne Bonny in the prison record. It is believed she was set free.

Calico Jack has been the inspiration of books, movies, and video games. The 2003 movie *Pirates of the Caribbean: Curse of the Black Pearl* uses

Calico Jack's flag of the skull and swords on the pirate ship, *The Black Pearl.*

It was easy to become a pirate too. Any ship was fair game. As Stede Bonnet found out, it was easy to obtain a fast ship, a poor crew that would do anything, and go "a pirating."[8]

THE GENTLEMAN PIRATE

Stede Bonnet was not always a pirate. He was a well-respected, well-educated gentleman who came from an English family. Bonnet owned a sugar plantation in Barbados. Many found it strange that a man who had so much would become a pirate. He was later called the gentleman pirate.

He bought his ship in 1717, which was unheard of among pirates. Why buy a ship when there were so many for the taking? He hired about seventy sailors in Barbados and snuck out of the harbor a few nights later.

Bonnet and his crew sailed north plundering ships. He went as far as the New England coast and decided to return. His crew realized that Bonnet was not a sailor at all. He did not know how to sail a ship or be a pirate. The crew became angry with Bonnet.

Bonnet harbored his ship in the Bay of Honduras. There he met Edward Teach, who by then was known as Blackbeard—the ruthless

Treasure Hunt - Microsoft Internet Explorer

File   Edit   View   Favorites   Tools   Help

Address http://whyfiles.org/036pirates/   Go   Links

ARGHH! TALES *from the* DEEP

Aye, There be Pirates Here

Archeologists think they've
found the wrecked flagship of a
scurvy pirate named Blackbeard.
That's got us lubbers wondering
what else might we find in Davy
Jones' Locker?

Set sail on the Queen Anne's
Revenge.

A lost city, perhaps?

Some ancient engineering plans?

A ship full of royal treasure?

How do
treasure

**Tales From
the Deep**

The "Why? Files" from the University of Wisconsin presents an illustrated look at pirates, pirate ships, and methods used in the search for treasure. The site also has a bibliography, glossary, and some links to other pirate-related sites.

Access this Web site from http://www.myreportlinks.com

pirate. The two became friends and decided to sail together. This was strange because Blackbeard was a true pirate and Bonnet was not. Many people wondered why Blackbeard would partner with Bonnet.

When this relationship ended just months later, an amnesty program was in place for pirates who agreed to stop their illegal activities. Bonnet surrendered to the governor of North Carolina, Charles Eden, to "take the King's pardon." But, still longing to be a pirate, Bonnet continued to capture ships. He was finally caught and hung for piracy in 1718.

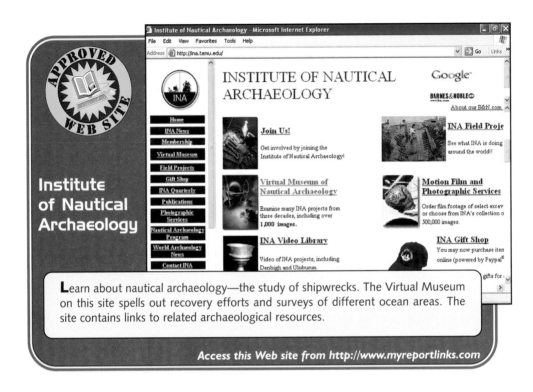

Learn about nautical archaeology—the study of shipwrecks. The Virtual Museum on this site spells out recovery efforts and surveys of different ocean areas. The site contains links to related archaeological resources.

Access this Web site from http://www.myreportlinks.com

SCAVENGERS OF THE SEA

The area of the Outer Banks was very dangerous for traveling, and remains so today. Diamond Shoals is where the Gulf Stream meets the Labrador Current. It is just off the coast of Hatteras Island. Sandbars unexpectedly appear in shallow waters. Strong currents, winds, and waves make it easy for a ship to sink. Many ships, including pirate ships, have been lost in this area.

People would come to the shoreline of Hatteras Island to collect parts of ships and find treasures. These treasures included rum, gold, furniture, silver, and more. The people who searched for treasures are often referred to as scavengers. They built shacks along the beach. What they couldn't use, the scavengers sold or bartered. Since money was not used at this time, people on the Outer Banks traded their goods for items like flour, oil, and meat products.

Even though the golden age of piracy lasted just thirty years, ships continued to sail this dangerous ocean off the North Carolina coast. Many sailors died on the rough waters, but still more people were drawn to the area.

Villages were established, and the ocean was a plentiful food source. Most settlers lived off the ocean's fish, and some brought in a few cows and pigs. It was not an easy life. The challenging weather made it difficult. Hurricanes and storms called nor'easters were common, and these storms destroyed many villages. But this did not drive the settlers away. Instead, they moved to higher ground and rebuilt.

As the villages grew on the Outer Banks, people became involved in other aspects of village life. A government was established and small businesses grew. The lifesaving business was one such business. All of the shipwrecks meant there were plenty of lives to be saved. Life stations, lighthouses, supply boats, post offices, and weather stations were constructed.

Chapter 3

Ocracoke Lighthouse was rebuilt in 1823. It is seventy-five feet tall, and its daymark identification is its all-white exterior.

Part Land, Part Sea

The government did not always protect Cape Hatteras. The barrier islands that make up the Outer Banks were changed when most of the trees were cut down in the sixteenth and seventeenth centuries. The trees were cut down in the wider areas of the Outer Banks. This drastically changed much of the landscape from a wooded paradise to a barren, sandy place. Today it is considered a sunny paradise by many beachgoers, although it would not be this way if the islands did not have some help.

In the early 1900s, many residents realized that their homes, businesses, and way of life should be protected. Small fishing communities were located on the Outer Banks. The constant threat of storms, wind, and waves blew sand all around. How could they keep the barrier islands stable? The best way to protect the Outer Banks was to make a barrier between the ocean and the land.

As mentioned in chapter 1, in 1930 the Civilian Conservation Corps (CCC) built a line that stretched up and down the beaches for miles. This line was made of sand that was piled up high to create a dune. The dune protected homes and businesses that lay just beyond it. The CCC added fences and vegetation to the dunes to provide extra fortification.

In some areas today, visitors will see large dunes with some vegetation. Sometimes they will see fences, which help to hold the sand back so it

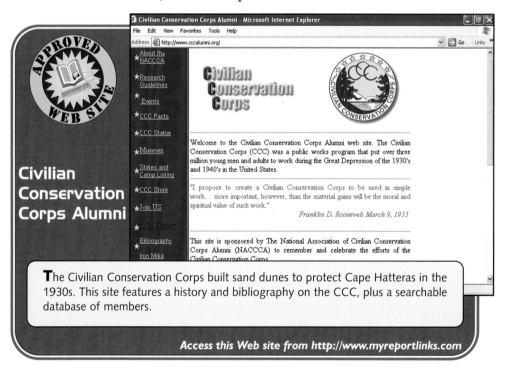

The Civilian Conservation Corps built sand dunes to protect Cape Hatteras in the 1930s. This site features a history and bibliography on the CCC, plus a searchable database of members.

Access this Web site from http://www.myreportlinks.com

doesn't blow over the road into parking lots and homes. Many sea oats were planted to help hold the sand down. Still, the ocean can break through the barrier—all it takes is a bad storm.

A Protected Area

Seeing a need to further protect valuable areas along the Outer Banks, the National Park Service—a federal government agency—stepped in. In 1953, Cape Hatteras National Seashore was declared a protected area. This upset many local residents. Because seventy-two miles of beautiful beach now belonged to the government, many bans were enacted. Suddenly some beaches were closed to the residents to protect the wildlife like loggerhead turtles and certain species of birds. Local residents felt that the National Park Service cared more about the wildlife than it did the citizens of the Outer Banks.

The government bought the land from the people and paid very little for it. This angered many residents. (At the time, the government paid fair market value; however, the value of land on the Outer Banks is much higher today.)

With the park came some big changes. The dirt roads were paved, bridges were built, and more people came to the area. Many local residents feel that the changes the National Park Service brought have drastically changed the Outer Banks.

Fences along the beach at Cape Hatteras serve as fortification to keep the sand from blowing away during storms.

Tourism increased, and millions of people now visit each year. Of course with people comes money. Businesses on the Outer Banks do well, especially during the summer months.

Some residents saw a need for change. They knew the Outer Banks needed help if it were to stay the same. By 1953, nearly seventeen thousand acres of land had been bought up. Some families who thought Cape Hatteras National Seashore was a good idea donated land. All the land obtained was given to the federal government.

FIRST SEASHORE PARK

Cape Hatteras National Seashore became the first seashore park in the United States. Today more than 2 million people visit Cape Hatteras National Seashore each year. Some residents of the Outer Banks are not happy with the National Park Service. Life has drastically changed on the barrier islands for some, but others consider it a good change.

The islands themselves have not changed much since the 1930s. The dune system seems to work well. Certain species are being saved from extinction. The tourism industry has brought in a great deal of income. Cape Hatteras National Seashore attracts visitors from all over the world not just to see its beaches, but to learn about the amazing history of the seashore and the Outer Banks.

SHIPWRECKED

A three-masted schooner sails quietly north. It is carrying goods from Charleston, South Carolina, to Baltimore, Maryland. Sugar, flour, coffee, salt, and spices are just some of the load. It is not a long journey, and the captain of the schooner has made it before.

One part of the trip always makes his stomach flip-flop. To the west lies the Outer Banks. To the east is the wide-open ocean. To the west, clouds thicken. The captain sees fork lightning brighten the sky and then disappear into the water. The horizon darkens and so does the deep water.

On land, there is no sign of life. The captain can only see a silhouette of the shoreline when the lightning flashes. There are no lighthouses, no fires on the beach. He cannot tell how close to the shore the ship is or where the danger lies. Suddenly, the captain has a decision to make. He knows he's in a bad spot and barks out commands to his crew. They prepare for rough sailing. They lower the sails and tie everything down.

As the storm approaches, strong winds rock the schooner. The winds push the schooner closer to shore. Waves crash over the top deck flooding the lower decks. The crew does everything it can to save the cargo, the ship, and everyone on board. But they cannot fight against Mother Nature. Some members of the crew huddle in a corner and pray. Others work hard for hours, bailing water. They rock and roll in the waves and hope for the best.

A loud creaking sound frightens the crew. The schooner suddenly jerks and tilts to the right. The main mast breaks in half from the sudden jolt. It dangles above, caught in the rigging. It can come crashing down at any moment. Waves and wind continue to pound the ship, but it does not rock as badly. The schooner has run aground. There is little the captain and his crew can do but wait for the storm to end and for help to come.

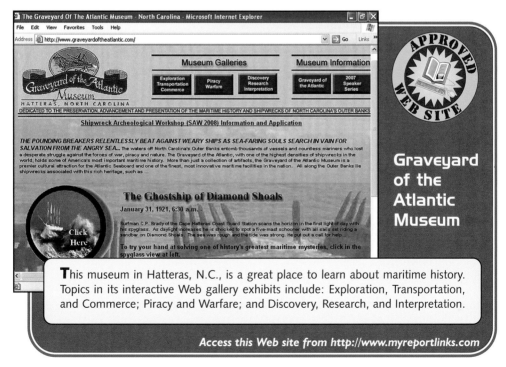

Graveyard of the Atlantic Museum

This museum in Hatteras, N.C., is a great place to learn about maritime history. Topics in its interactive Web gallery exhibits include: Exploration, Transportation, and Commerce; Piracy and Warfare; and Discovery, Research, and Interpretation.

Access this Web site from http://www.myreportlinks.com

⮕ CLASHING CURRENTS

This area is so perilous for sea travel because of two currents that crash into each other just off the coast of Cape Hatteras and Cape Hatteras National Seashore. The Gulf Stream is a strong, warm current moving from the south to north. A cold current from the Arctic moves north to south. This is called the Labrador Current. The two currents meet just off the North Carolina coast.

The area called Diamond Shoals is where the currents have the greatest impact. Diamond Shoals is about eight miles off the coast of Cape Hatteras. The waves make sandbars, which move and change all the time. Many ships run aground on these sandbars only to be lost at sea forever.

Sailors call this area the Graveyard of the Atlantic. It runs along the entire North Carolina coast from Cape Lookout and Cape Fear in the south all the way to Nags Head. Sailors who wanted to move their cargo up and down the coast had no choice but to sail along the North Carolina coast. It was faster and cheaper to sail close to the coastline. The Gulf Stream actually made travel faster by carrying ships quickly along the coast.

There are thought to have been about one thousand shipwrecks in this area, dating as far back as the late 1500s. The ship *Tiger* of Sir

Richard Greenville's expedition was wrecked in 1585. The *Lois Joyce* is one of the most recent shipwrecks. It was a one-hundred-foot fishing trawler that ran aground in 1981.

The *Lois Joyce* was trying to enter Oregon Outlet during a storm in December. A Coast Guard helicopter rescued the crew, but the ship sank. The wreck can still be seen and is best viewed at low tide. Even with modern-day equipment and working lighthouses, ships and boats continue to run into problems along the North Carolina coast.

USS MONITOR SHIPWRECK

Famous shipwrecks are not always pirate ships laden with treasure. Some famous shipwrecks off the coast of North Carolina occurred in the last 150 years.

During the Civil War, shipping lanes off the North Carolina coast were used by both the North and the South. It was not a safe place to sail. For the first three years of the war, the only ships that traveled here were those bringing supplies to the troops.

Naval warfare would play an important role in the Civil War. Stronger ships were soon built not only with wood but by using iron as well. These new ships were called ironclad ships. When Virginia seceded from the Union in April 1861, the federal navy burned and sank the USS *Merrimack,* a steam frigate docked in Virginia. They wanted to prevent the South from using it against them. However, the Confederate navy salvaged the wooden ship, repaired it, and turned it into an ironclad. They renamed it the CSS *Virginia*.[1]

The North took it one step further. Instead of using a wooden ship, they built an ironclad ship— a ship built entirely of iron. It was also one of the first steamships ever built.[2] The *Monitor* was the North's "secret weapon."

The CSS *Virginia* and the *Monitor* fought at Hampton Roads, Virginia. This was the first battle of its kind, pitting two ironclad ships against one another. It was a critical battle, as Hampton Roads

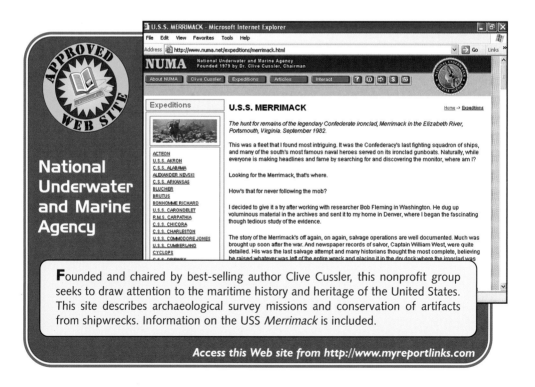

National Underwater and Marine Agency

Founded and chaired by best-selling author Clive Cussler, this nonprofit group seeks to draw attention to the maritime history and heritage of the United States. This site describes archaeological survey missions and conservation of artifacts from shipwrecks. Information on the USS *Merrimack* is included.

Access this Web site from http://www.myreportlinks.com

was a waterway that offered direct access to the Confederate capital of Richmond, Virginia.

While the battle at Hampton Roads was technically a tie or "draw," the *Monitor* did succeed in preventing the Confederacy from gaining control of this important waterway. After two months and many confrontations, the CSS *Virginia* ran aground in the shallow waters of the James River.[3] Rather than allowing the ship to fall into enemy hands, the crew abandoned it and set it on fire.

The *Monitor* had helped the North secure Hampton Roads and won a battle at Drewry's Bluff in Virginia. No longer needed, the *Monitor* was on its way to South Carolina. It was December 30, 1862. Another ship, the *Rhode Island,* sailed with it. The crew of the *Rhode Island* attached a towline to the *Monitor.* This way, the *Monitor* could move faster.

THE *MONITOR'S* LAST VOYAGE

As they were rounding Cape Hatteras, the ships were caught in a storm. "The sea pitched together in the peculiar manner only seen at Hatteras. . . . [I]t rolled over us as if our vessel were a rock in the ocean only a few inches above the water," said helmsman Francis B. Butts.[4] The coal that powered the engines became wet, and it was hard to keep the fires burning. Engines were slowed and

▲ *A depiction of the critical Civil War battle between the USS* Merrimack *(renamed the CSS* Virginia*) and the USS* Monitor *at Hampton Roads, Virginia in 1862.*

orders were given to operate only the pumps, which got rid of the water.

The towline between the two ships had to be cut. Without a strong engine, the *Monitor* could easily crash into the *Rhode Island.* Two men were swept overboard. The second man, John Stocking, managed to cut the tow rope before he drowned. The pumps soon failed. The crew had to bail out the water. Despite their efforts, the *Monitor* was taking on too much water.

The crew decided to leave the ship. Two rescue boats were launched from the *Rhode Island.* They saved most of the men on the *Monitor,* but some were left behind. One boat was able to get the men back on the *Rhode Island.* Those on the other boat remembered the men who were still awaiting help on the *Monitor.* They went back to rescue them, but by now the *Monitor* was about two miles away. As the *Monitor* sank, there was no sign of the small lifeboat either.

The *Monitor* was located in 1974. On January 30, 1975, it was made the nation's first marine sanctuary. The Mariners' Museum in Newport

Visit the site of **The Mariners' Museum** to see a full-scale replica of the historic ironclad ship USS *Monitor,* and watch a 3-D video reenactment of its sinking. The museum's USS *Monitor* Center, newly opened in 2007, has more than a thousand artifacts from the ship, and its Web site has numerous interactive online exhibitions.

News, Virginia, has more than one thousand artifacts retrieved from the ship.

U-BOATS OFF THE COAST!

Imagine being closer to war off the coast of North Carolina than most American troops who were serving overseas. During World War II, from 1939 to 1945, German U-boats were often seen off the coast of Cape Hatteras. U-boats were submarines. After the attack at Pearl Harbor, Hitler ordered a submarine attack on the East Coast shipping lanes of the United States.[5]

Early in the morning of January 18, 1942, just sixty miles off the coast of Cape Hatteras, a tanker named the *Allan Jackson* loaded with crude oil was struck by torpedoes and sank. This was the first submarine attack off the coast of North Carolina. Many ships would meet the same fate. In three months, the Nazis had sunk about fifty large ships. But things would soon change.

On April 14, 1942, the destroyer *Roper* opened fire and sank the German submarine, U-85. A total of eighty-seven U.S. ships were lost to U-boat attacks off the Carolina coast.

SAVING LIVES

Because of all the shipwrecks off the Outer Banks, another industry came about. It was the industry of saving lives. Long ago, when scavengers combed the beaches for treasures, they also found people—some were dead, some alive. This happened when there was a shipwreck. If the wreck could be seen from shore, brave men would risk their own lives to save others. Sometimes men would swim out to rescue people or would launch a boat. America's first volunteer lifesaving stations were huts built by the Massachusetts Humane Society in 1787.

Lighthouses were built along the eastern seacoast, but the ones on the Outer Banks were not built until the nineteenth century. It took a while for lifesaving stations to be constructed on the Outer Banks. By 1874, there were seven stations. Within two years, twenty-nine more were built so that every seven miles along the Outer Banks, there was a lifesaving station.

⊝ SOLDIERS OF THE SURF

These stations served several purposes. They housed the men who served, the boats used to save mariners, and those who were rescued. The men who worked so hard to save the lives of many were often referred to as "Soldiers of the Surf" or "Storm Warriors."

One of the few original lifesaving stations that remains today is found at Chicamacomico in Rodanthe, on Cape Hatteras. Built in 1874, it was the first lifesaving station in North Carolina, and it

▲ One of the buildings at the Chicamacomico lifesaving station built at Rodanthe in 1874.

remained active until 1954. Many lives were saved along the Outer Banks because of the heroic efforts of the men who manned such lifesaving stations. When the U.S. Coast Guard was founded in 1915, the U.S. Life-Saving Service became part of the Coast Guard.

➲ LIGHTSHIPS

Lighthouses were desperately needed along the coastline of the Outer Banks. With all the shipwrecks that occurred, mariners needed to know where the dangerous areas were. Lightships were used too, especially around Diamond Shoals, one of the most treacherous places located along the Outer Banks.

The lightships were anchored in these perilous areas. They would shine a bright light to warn ships to stay away. The first lightship was called *Cape Hatteras*. It was put in place in 1824, and remained until 1827. This lightship survived three storms, although the third storm pushed it into Ocracoke Beach. Even though lightships were anchored in place, they often broke away from their moorings in bad weather.

Life on a lightship was often lonely. In 1825, Captain Holden brought his entire family to live on the lightship with him. He lived with his wife, three daughters, and a small crew on the lightship for two years. During a hurricane in August 1827,

▲ *The Diamond Shoal lightship #69 shown stranded on the beach at Cape Hatteras.*

the lightship ran aground. Captain Holden and his family survived with a lot of bumps and bruises.

There was a strong need for a lighthouse at Cape Hatteras and along the Outer Banks. The first lighthouse at Cape Hatteras was built in 1803. However, because Cape Hatteras Light did not work well, it could not completely take the place of lightships. Lightships were still used as warning devices through the middle of the twentieth century.[6]

HATTERAS LIGHT

By the end of the eighteenth century, hundreds of ships had been wrecked off the coast of Cape Hatteras. Mariners demanded that a lighthouse be put in place. In October 1803, Cape Hatteras Light was built. It was ninety feet tall and made of sandstone. It was a welcome sight to mariners—when it worked. But many complained they could not see the small light, which was fueled by sperm whale oil. It could not be seen far out by Diamond Shoals where it would be most helpful.

A group of people called the Lighthouse Board decided that the tower should be made taller and a new light put in place. The tower was then

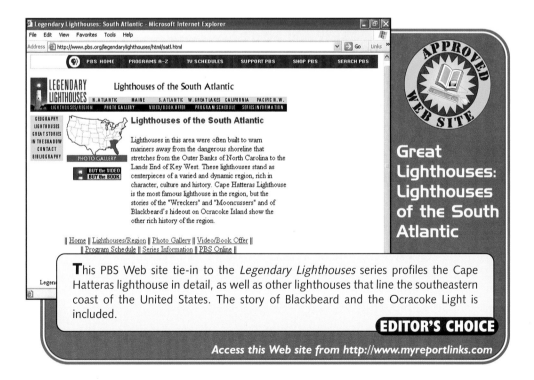

Great Lighthouses: Lighthouses of the South Atlantic

This PBS Web site tie-in to the *Legendary Lighthouses* series profiles the Cape Hatteras lighthouse in detail, as well as other lighthouses that line the southeastern coast of the United States. The story of Blackbeard and the Ocracoke Light is included.

EDITOR'S CHOICE

Access this Web site from http://www.myreportlinks.com

raised to one hundred and fifty feet. A Fresnel lens was installed too. The glass Fresnel lens magnified the small light so that it could be more easily seen from the water.[7]

The Civil War took place from 1861 to 1865. When the Confederate troops left the area, they took the Fresnel lens with them. The lighthouse itself was in great need of repair. It was decided that instead of repairing it, a new lighthouse would be built. Beach erosion played a role in where the new light would be located.

In 1870, the new lighthouse was built six hundred feet back from the original light and sixteen hundred feet from the shoreline. It is the tallest brick lighthouse in the United States, towering at 208 feet. The spiral stripes in black and white set it apart from all other lighthouses. The stripes on the Cape Hatteras Light, as with other North Carolina lighthouses, act as a daytime identification mark, or daymark.

➲A MONUMENTAL MOVE

Imagine moving a lighthouse! This may seem impossible, but in 1999, the National Park Service had a difficult decision to make. Move the Cape Hatteras Light, or try to keep the ocean from destroying it. Although many local residents wanted to keep the lighthouse at its original location, beach erosion had already forced it to be moved back six hundred feet in 1870. More than one hundred years later, the same problem was reoccurring. Only now, the ocean was just one hundred and twenty feet away. Residents could not stop the ocean from creeping closer to the lighthouse. It had to be saved.

The lighthouse was carefully lifted and moved very slowly along a seventy-foot-wide path. It took about three weeks to move it 2,900 feet. Along with the lighthouse, the keeper's quarters and the oil house were also moved. (The oil house is where the oil supply for fuel to make the light used to be kept.) It was a monumental undertaking. Today, the lighthouse sits far enough away from the ocean but close enough to still do its job and warn mariners of danger. Visitors can also climb the tower and enjoy the view.

OCRACOKE LIGHT

Ocracoke Light is nestled among homes and trees. It is located on the southern tip of Cape Hatteras National Seashore on Ocracoke Island. The only way to get there is by a ferry. Winding roads in the small town lead to this second-oldest operating lighthouse in the United States. Sandy Hook Lighthouse in New Jersey, first lit in 1764, is the oldest operating lighthouse. Ocracoke Light is the oldest operating lighthouse in North Carolina.

The Cape Hatteras Lighthouse is shown being reunited with its keepers quarters, bottom left, as it reaches the end of its move inland on July 7, 1999. The lighthouse traveled 2,900 feet from its former location, where it stood precariously close to the Atlantic's booming waves.

The original Ocracoke lighthouse was built in 1794 on nearby Shell Castle Island. It helped mariners sail through a deep inlet channel between Pamlico Sound and the Atlantic Ocean, and it operated for almost thirty years. But when the channel moved, the light was of no use. Then, in 1818, lightning destroyed the lighthouse.

In 1822, the government bought two acres of land on Ocracoke and built the current lighthouse. It was designed by Noah Porter from Massachusetts and finished in 1823. The lighthouse is not tall compared to the one at Cape Hatteras; it is only seventy-five feet high. The entire exterior of the lighthouse is painted white. This is its daymark identification.

Like the other lighthouses on Cape Hatteras National Seashore, Ocracoke Light encountered trouble during the Civil War. Members of the Confederate army dismantled the Fresnel light. Fortunately, the Union army was able to put it back together.

Ocracoke Light cannot be climbed. But visitors may take the short walk to the light, take pictures, and enjoy the beauty that surrounds this historic landmark.

→ Bodie Light

A black-and-white-striped lighthouse is located on Bodie Island. It was the third lighthouse built along Cape Hatteras National Seashore. Because of the dangerous waters off the coast, a third lighthouse was needed to help mariners navigate around Cape Hatteras.

The current Bodie Light is not the original tower. A fifty-four-foot tower was first built in 1846, but it started leaning and could not be used. Then an eighty-foot-tall tower was built. When the Confederate army lost its hold on the Outer Banks during the Civil War in 1861, it blew up the tower. In 1871, a new lighthouse and light keeper's home were constructed, and began operating in 1872.

Bodie Light stands 156 feet tall. It still operates, too. The National Park Service owns it. Visitors cannot climb the lighthouse, but they can enter the visitor's center and learn all about the interesting history of Bodie Light.

Chapter 4

A white ibis, one of more than two hundred species of shorebirds that may be found at Pea Island National Wildlife Refuge.

Bubble Holes and Barking Sand

Sand is an important part of Cape Hatteras National Seashore and the surrounding area. After all, it is everywhere. Many visitors come just for the sandy beaches that stretch on for miles. There is nothing like spending a day at the beach. The sand warms under the hot sun. The ocean greets swimmers and fishermen, and the sea breeze is soothing.

The beach and dunes are part of an interesting ecosystem. Many animals and sea creatures make their home in this area. There are other places that are also unique to Cape Hatteras National Seashore. These include Pea Island and the maritime forests. No matter where a person goes on

Cape Hatteras National Seashore, he or she will see some interesting wildlife.

⊜ PLENTY OF FISH

The ocean plays a huge role in how the beach is formed and the types of plants and animals that live there. It is a rough place to live, and only certain kinds of creatures and plant life can survive.

The ocean is filled with life. Because Cape Hatteras National Seashore sticks way out in the ocean, fish are plentiful. People come from all over to fish in the quiet inlets or out at sea. This is called deep-sea fishing. But most anglers surf fish. Surf fishing is done from the beach. On any given day along Cape Hatteras National Seashore,

N.C. Wildlife Resources Commission: Fishing

Fishing is very popular at Cape Hatteras. This site spells out when and where you can fish in North Carolina, describes stocking programs, and features "Ask a Biologist" and Q&A sections.

Access this Web site from http://www.myreportlinks.com

fishing lines are cast into the ocean. Anglers patiently wait for the catch of the day.

➔A VARIETY OF SEA CREATURES

Anglers will catch all kinds of fish, including blue-fish, Spanish mackerel, cobia, bonito, speckled trout, sea mullet, striped bass, and flounder. The fish that many anglers want to catch is the red drum, also known as the channel bass. It is North Carolina's state fish.

Fish come in close to the shore. Some swimmers will feel fish rub up against them, but most are harmless. Shark attacks are rare, and so are shark sightings. In the last three hundred years, fewer than twenty shark attacks have occurred in North Carolina.[1] Sharks may be rare, but it is common to see a pod of dolphins just offshore.

Stingrays swim offshore too. Sometimes they can be seen jumping out of the water, and swimmers have to be careful not to step on them. Stingrays hide in the sand, making it difficult to see them. They have a sharp barb that can be very painful if you step on it.

Jellyfish float on top of the water, and most do not sting. Jellyfish with clear bodies are often harmless, but those with pink or blue coloring should be avoided. The Portuguese man-of-war is a dangerous type of jellyfish found in the waters of Cape Hatteras National Seashore.

Sometimes dead sea creatures will wash up during storms. These may include horseshoe crabs, fish, and even whales.

LIFE IN THE SWASH ZONE

The beaches and dunes that make up much of Cape Hatteras National Seashore are both beautiful and fun. The beach is divided into different areas in which plants and animals live.

Swash is the part of the wave that rolls gently onto the beach. The swash zone is the area of beach that the wave rolls over. Many microscopic creatures live in this zone between grains of sand. Other smaller creatures live there too. These include sand fleas, also called mole crabs, and coquina clams.

Larger beach creatures include worms, clams, crabs, birds, and turtles. Worms, coquina clams, and mole crabs provide plenty of food for birds and fish. For the beach stroller, they are not always easy to see. Many of these beach dwellers can burrow into the sand quickly.

BUBBLE HOLES

The sand is filled with air. When the tide comes in, waves crash on the beach and create the swash zone. As the waves retreat, tiny holes appear. Most people think these are air holes made by animals living in the sand, but they are not. Small air pockets in the sand fill with water as the tide comes in. When the tide goes back out, the water is replaced by air between the grains of sand. Sometimes bubbles form as the wave returns to sea. The small holes are also called nail holes because they are no bigger than the diameter of a nail.

BARKING SAND

Does sand bark or sing? Often visitors to the beach will notice that as they step, the sand seems to be making a noise. To some it sounds like a bark, to others a squeak. Barking sand occurs at beaches all over the world. It happens at Cape Hatteras National Seashore on the upper part of the beach where the sand is drier. Barking sand is known by several other names as well, including musical sand or squeaking sand. In Japan, it is called frog-sound sand.

The noise is produced when a layer of sand grains slides or rubs over another layer of sand grains. When a person steps just right on the surface of the sand, it makes a funny noise. The best barks or songs come from medium-size grains of sand like those found on Cape Hatteras.[2]

NATURAL TREASURES

The beach at Cape Hatteras National Seashore is a treasure chest. Occasionally, a shipwreck will

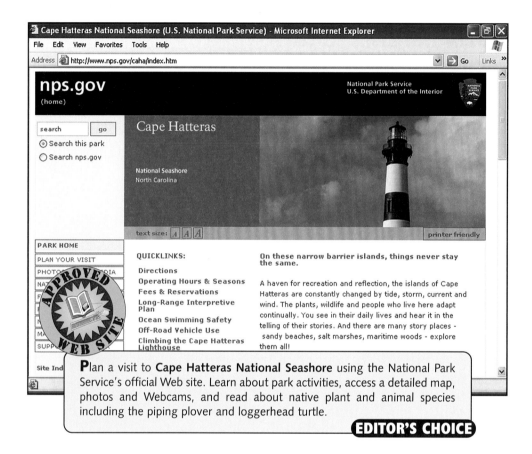

Cape Hatteras National Seashore (U.S. National Park Service) - Microsoft Internet Explorer

File   Edit   View   Favorites   Tools   Help

Address http://www.nps.gov/caha/index.htm

nps.gov
(home)

National Park Service
U.S. Department of the Interior

search   go
⦿ Search this park
◯ Search nps.gov

Cape Hatteras

National Seashore
North Carolina

text size: A A A   printer friendly

PARK HOME

PLAN YOUR VISIT

PHOTO...   ...DIA

NA...

F...

N...

M...

SUPP...

Site Ind...

QUICKLINKS:

Directions

Operating Hours & Seasons

Fees & Reservations

Long-Range Interpretive Plan

Ocean Swimming Safety

Off-Road Vehicle Use

Climbing the Cape Hatteras Lighthouse

On these narrow barrier islands, things never stay the same.

A haven for recreation and reflection, the islands of Cape Hatteras are constantly changed by tide, storm, current and wind. The plants, wildlife and people who live here adapt continually. You see in their daily lives and hear it in the telling of their stories. And there are many story places - sandy beaches, salt marshes, maritime woods - explore them all!

Plan a visit to **Cape Hatteras National Seashore** using the National Park Service's official Web site. Learn about park activities, access a detailed map, photos and Webcams, and read about native plant and animal species including the piping plover and loggerhead turtle.

EDITOR'S CHOICE

wash up to shore but not often. Some of the best treasures come from the ocean, and everyone can enjoy them. Shells, fossils, sand dollars, starfish and sharks' teeth are just some of the treasures that beachcombers will find.

Many of the shells found on the beaches at Cape Hatteras National Seashore are, in fact, fossils. They are hundreds to thousands of years old. These fossils come from snail and clam shells and some corals. Much of the sand is made from fossils too.

After an animal dies, its shell ends up on the beach. Most of the shells found there today are not from animals that died recently. Instead, they are from animals that died thousands of years ago. Once in a while, fossils of extinct creatures that lived millions of years ago will also wash up on shore. Giant oysters from the Miocene period (23 to 5.3 million years ago) have been found. They are three times the size of today's oysters.

SHELL HASH AND SHARKS' TEETH

Another common sight on the beach is horseshoe crab shells. Many people think they are the dead bodies of horseshoe crabs. In fact, a horseshoe crab sheds its shell and grows a new one. It also builds its nest in the sand to lay its eggs.

Shell hash is commonly seen on the beaches. Shell hash is made up of small pieces of shells that have been rolling around in the waves. They are smooth, rounded, and fun to collect. If they are left alone, the shells will eventually become tiny grains of sand.

Sharks' teeth can also be found on the beaches of Cape Hatteras National Seashore. Topsail Island is a good place to find them. Most of the teeth date back to the Miocene period and are washed up on shore like shells. These shiny black teeth are fossils. Most people find them when scooping

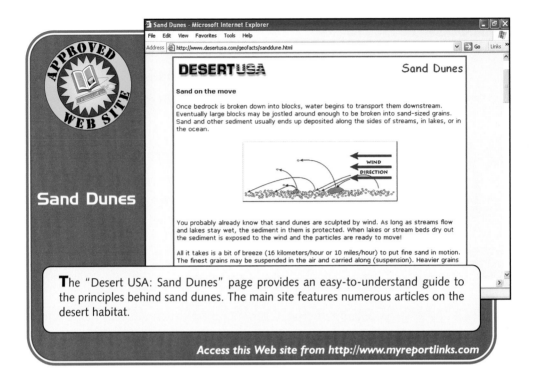

Sand Dunes

DESERT USA — Sand Dunes

Sand on the move

Once bedrock is broken down into blocks, water begins to transport them downstream. Eventually large blocks may be jostled around enough to be broken into sand-sized grains. Sand and other sediment usually ends up deposited along the sides of streams, in lakes, or in the ocean.

You probably already know that sand dunes are sculpted by wind. As long as streams flow and lakes stay wet, the sediment in them is protected. When lakes or stream beds dry out the sediment is exposed to the wind and the particles are ready to move!

All it takes is a bit of breeze (16 kilometers/hour or 10 miles/hour) to put fine sand in motion. The finest grains may be suspended in the air and carried along (suspension). Heavier grains

The "Desert USA: Sand Dunes" page provides an easy-to-understand guide to the principles behind sand dunes. The main site features numerous articles on the desert habitat.

Access this Web site from http://www.myreportlinks.com

up shell hash or searching through broken pieces of shell.

The dunes along Cape Hatteras National Seashore were not always in place as they are now. Smaller dunes existed along the beach, but they were not continuous. Sand was brought in to build larger dunes, which are now continuous along Cape Hatteras National Seashore. These dunes were built to protect the homes and property on the barrier islands and to help slow beach erosion.

The wind, which always blows here, is constantly changing the size, shape, and look of the dunes. To help control the shifting sands, dune grass was planted. North Carolina farmers are encouraged to grow dune plants. Many times, storms will ruin a dune or kill the plants. There is always a need to grow and plant new vegetation. In 2002, 2 million dune plants were planted.[3]

Dune grass is also called sea oats. It tolerates the salty sea spray and high winds, and keeps the sand from blowing. It grows in clumps and does not spread well. People have also planted American beach grass, which is similar to dune grass,

▲ Sea oats, a hardy plant also called dune grass, partially hide a view of the Cape Hatteras lighthouse.

but spreads better. Flowers such as dotted horsemint, wild morning glories, and Indian blankets grow in the dunes. The Indian blanket, a bright red flower with yellow tips, is also called fire wheel. It grows best in dry, sandy areas.

Some animals found in the dunes include snakes and other reptiles, rabbits, and crabs. Holes the size of a half dollar can be seen in the dunes and down on the upper beach. These holes are burrows made by ghost crabs.

⊝ EYES ON THE SKIES

Cape Hatteras National Seashore and the surrounding areas are home to many species of birds. The variety of habitats makes it one of the best areas to bird-watch. Many birds live here year-round, while others use the area as a resting place on their long journeys south or north. The ocean, ponds, marshes, and sounds provide ample food and shelter for birds. More than four hundred species of birds have been seen here, including pelicans, woodpeckers, kinglets, gulls, piping plovers, and marsh wrens. The three places along Cape Hatteras National Seashore that are best for bird-watching are Bodie Island, Pea Island National Wildlife Refuge, and Cape Point.

Bodie Island is the northernmost part of Cape Hatteras National Seashore. This area has several

▲ The piping plover, a small shorebird that resembles a sandpiper, builds its nests along sandy beaches of the Atlantic coast. Various predators as well as development are threatening its habitat and breeding grounds.

different habitats that attract birds. The north end of the island is marshy and flat, but it is an ideal place to see birds like herons and egrets. On occasion, eagles and owls can also be spotted. Coquina Beach is another good place to see birds like loons, which may be seen in the winter months, and a variety of ducks.

There is a pond and pine groves near the Bodie Lighthouse. A large variety of waterfowl can be spotted here, depending on the season. While

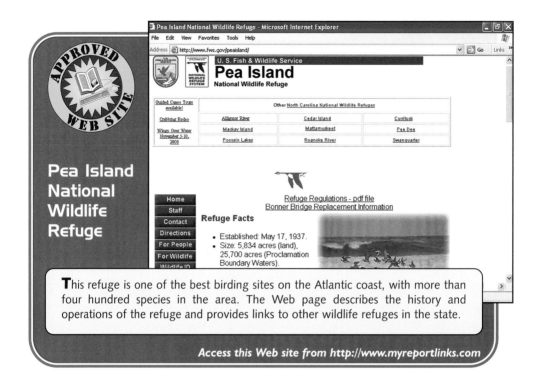

This refuge is one of the best birding sites on the Atlantic coast, with more than four hundred species in the area. The Web page describes the history and operations of the refuge and provides links to other wildlife refuges in the state.

Access this Web site from http://www.myreportlinks.com

hiking through the paths on the Bodie Island Dike Trail, which passes the pond, a visitor may encounter songbirds, wading birds in the creek, and raptors. And the beach and flats around Oregon Inlet are a great place to watch piping plovers, sandpipers, and terns.

The piping plover, a type of bird in the area, is a species that is threatened. Its habitat is being destroyed because of all the building, erosion, and pollution. Native and non-native predators have reduced its numbers. Cats, raccoons, foxes, gulls, and mink hunt and kill the piping plover.

The piping plover prefers the beach. It lays its eggs right on top of the sand, and it does not build a nest. Since the eggs and chicks are sand colored, it is hard to see them. Their color helps to camouflage them from predators, but they are often stepped on or crushed by vehicles. The park service does rope off certain areas to help protect this threatened bird.

➔ BEST SITES FOR BIRD-WATCHING

Pea Island National Wildlife Refuge is one of the best birding sites on the Atlantic coast. It includes a large variety of habitats such as beaches, ponds, marshes, and dunes, and it is home to many local birds. It is a pit stop for migratory birds too. Snow geese, Canada geese, tundra swan, and ducks stop here to rest before heading farther south.

Cape Point is not easy to get to, but it is another great place to watch birds at Cape Hatteras National Seashore. The point is at the tip of Cape Hatteras and sticks out into the ocean. As Pat Moore, the director of the Cape Hatteras Bird Club, says, "The Point is like having a buffet of bird sightings laid out for you year-round."[4] It is home to piping plovers, black skimmers, American oystercatchers, gulls, and many more birds. Buxton Woods Nature Trail is another place to see land birds like sparrows, wrens, and warblers.

Each year, the area hosts a festival called *Wings Over Water.* It celebrates the wildlife found at Cape Hatteras National Seashore and the surrounding

The loggerhead turtle constructs its nests right on the beach in Cape Hatteras. The turtle is endangered due to factors such as pollution.

area. People can learn more about the wildlife and take bird-watching tours.

→ THE ENDANGERED LOGGERHEAD

Many types of sea turtles are found off the coast of Cape Hatteras National Seashore, where some use the beaches to lay their eggs. These include the loggerhead and Atlantic leatherback. Sadly, their numbers have greatly declined. The loggerhead is classified as endangered under the United States Endangered Species Act, while the leatherback is critically endangered. North Carolina has the second highest rate of sea turtle death of all the U.S. coastal states. Texas is number one.[5]

Some natural causes affect the sea turtle's mortality rate, but unfortunately human activities do more damage. The nesting areas used by the turtles are also used by humans, and there is pollution in the water. Scientists and concerned people are trying to help the sea turtles by creating areas only for the turtles and also by educating people. Some beaches have started volunteer sea turtle groups.

The loggerhead is the most common of the sea turtles in this area, and it makes about a hundred nests on the beaches. A female loggerhead lays about a hundred eggs in a nest between August and October. The babies hatch in November. They are on their own right away, and they must make their way back to the water. Unfortunately, many don't succeed, and sea animals often eat those that do. It is believed that only one in a thousand sea turtles survives to adulthood.

→ TREES AND VEGETATION

Why are there so few trees along Cape Hatteras National Seashore? And why are those trees that are there so short? Trees and shrubs have a hard time growing on the barrier islands. The wind is constantly blowing, and it also carries salt, picked up from the ocean. The salt in the wind blows on the plants and scorches them. This keeps them from growing.

Some areas do have trees. The trees that do grow here are back from the beach, where the elevation is slightly higher. Pine trees, which do well in sand, tend to grow better in these areas. They are not as affected by the salty winds.

The woods that are found on the islands are called the maritime woods. They grow at the wider sections of the islands. Much of the barrier islands are flat, dry, and brown with little vegetation. The vegetation that does grow on the seashore, like sea oats and marsh grass, has to be able to thrive in wind and salt all year.

Chapter 5

Clouds build before a storm at Cape Hatteras.

Extreme Impact

The wind howls. The ocean lashes out like hands grabbing at the beach, boats, and buildings. The Outer Banks is not a safe place when a hurricane hits because the area sits out in the ocean. Nothing can protect the barrier islands. Most people are forced to evacuate when a major hurricane hits. They wait it out on the mainland, away from the ocean. But the islands and the many animals that live there cannot leave. The animals have to seek shelter and try to survive.

The Outer Banks and Cape Hatteras National Seashore is an area vulnerable to extreme impact. Hurricanes are just one way the islands are harmed each year. But the forces of nature cannot be stopped. The other extreme impact is development. With more people come more homes and businesses, and this is harmful to these narrow islands.

⇥CANNOT STOP NATURE

The Atlantic hurricane season starts on June 1 and ends on November 30. Yet many feel the summer season is the best time of the year to visit Cape Hatteras National Seashore. Vacationers come from all over the world to relax and enjoy the scenery. The fall is the best time to fish. Since hurricane season peaks in September, many hurricanes occur after the busy summer season is over.

A hurricane is a type of tropical cyclone. It develops far out in the Atlantic Ocean and gains

Hurricanes are a cause for concern in the Cape Hatteras area. This Web site promotes preparedness, provides news on hurricanes, and features links to updates from the National Hurricane Center. Its *Hurricanes 101* section describes how hurricanes occur and how they are classified.

Access this Web site from http://www.myreportlinks.com

strength as it crosses over warmer waters. It starts as a tropical depression and then develops into a tropical storm. By the time it is classified as a hurricane, winds have reached seventy-four miles per hour.

On the Outer Banks, wind causes a great deal of damage to homes. It can blow shingles off of roofs, knock down signs, and blow debris around. This flying debris can be very dangerous to people outside. But the biggest threat to the Outer Banks is the water surge. This is a huge wall of water that pushes onto the coast when a hurricane makes landfall. It floods homes and can even move them off their foundations.

Hurricanes are so powerful they can actually change the islands. Sand and water can close one inlet and open another. Beach erosion is another serious problem. Often when a major hurricane hits, the beach is eroded, or swept away.

➔ GREAT STORMS OF THE PAST

Hurricanes have been recorded on Hatteras Island since 1837. Back then, no one had televisions, phones, or radios to hear a storm warning. Often people were caught off guard, especially those on ships.

Racer's Storm, on October 8, 1837, was a very powerful hurricane. To some, it was the worst maritime disaster in North Carolina history. Two

▲ A new inlet one-third of a mile long was created by Hurricane Isabel in September 2003. The "Isabel Inlet" was later filled in by a massive rebuilding effort.

ships, the *Enterprise* and the *Home,* were just off the coast of the Outer Banks when they sank. As people tried to get off the sinking ships, lifeboats were overturned. One ship was equipped with only two life preservers, even though the ship carried 130 people. Forty people survived the storm and shipwreck. Most who died were women and children.

⇨ DEVASTATING STORMS

In July 1842, another storm grounded fourteen ships. Two ships sank with all of their crew members. The names of the ships and crew members were not recorded, so it is difficult to confirm how many lives were lost.

In 1846, a great flood formed Oregon Inlet and Hatteras Inlet. A northeast wind blew for two weeks, raising the water level so high that it flooded the areas between Hatteras and Frisco villages. This area once had much vegetation. Now it was under water. Many people were forced to find safety on higher sand hills.

Hatteras Island was devastated by a hurricane in 1899. It was so severe that groups of people would huddle in one house, only to have to flee for their lives. The water rose so high that many had to swim to the next house for safety. Livestock drowned, ships were wrecked, and the fishing industry was wiped out. "All of the bridges and footways over the creeks and small streams were swept away, and passing from one portion of the island to the other had to be done by boat. The road ways were piled from three to ten feet high with wreckage."[1]

⇨ HURRICANES OF THE FUTURE

The barrier islands are a long stretch of sandbars. They are not connected to land and are always

▲ A NOAA (National and Atmospheric Administration) satellite image of Hurricane Isabel close to making landfall on September 18, 2003.

shifting. It is easy for a hurricane to change the islands—sometimes drastically. In June 2004, a study conducted by geologists at Louisiana State University showed the Outer Banks was one of the three most likely places for a Category 5 hurricane to hit.[2]

A Category 5 hurricane is the strongest hurricane measured on the Saffir-Simpson scale. Winds are greater than 155 miles per hour, and the water surge can be as high as eighteen feet. Hurricanes tend to use the Gulf Stream as their guide. Its warm waters help move hurricanes up the coast. It also makes them stronger. This is not good news for the Outer Banks, which are frequently hit by tropical storms and hurricanes. On average, the Outer Banks experience a major hurricane about every four years.

Fortunately, the Outer Banks have never experienced a hurricane of Category 5 magnitude. If they do, life there will be forever changed. Cape Hatteras National Seashore would be destroyed. The man-made dunes will be completely washed and blown away. Beach erosion will be great, and the loss of homes and businesses will be huge. A fifteen- to eighteen-foot sea surge would completely flood the islands, causing them to disappear from the coastline.[3] What would likely remain of the Outer Banks would be sandbars seen only at low tide.

⊖ BEACH NOURISHMENT

The beaches on the Outer Banks, including Cape Hatteras National Seashore, are in great danger. Beach erosion, beach nourishment, and development threaten the beaches daily. Some people might think that strengthening a beach is a good idea. Beach nourishment is the practice of replacing sand that has been taken away by storms.

This is done by bringing in sand from other areas. But the sand brought in is not of the same consistency as the sand on the Outer Bank's beaches. In time, much of the original sand is gone or changed.

North Carolina beaches used to be brown in color, but now many places are not. The new sand has a different texture and look. To many people, it does not seem like the same beach. Two beaches on the Outer Banks have been changed. When new sand was brought in for one beach, it was too shelly. Another beach now has grapefruit-size rocks that make it hard to swim. These rocks also make it difficult for turtles to nest.

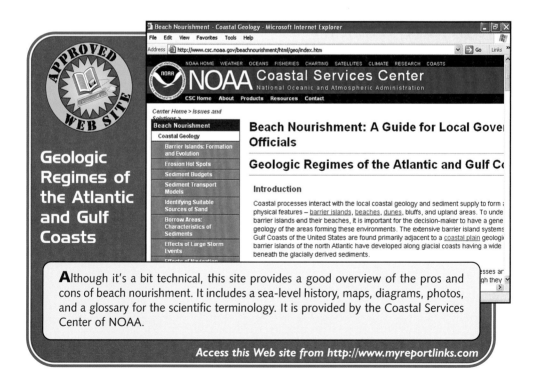

Geologic Regimes of the Atlantic and Gulf Coasts

Although it's a bit technical, this site provides a good overview of the pros and cons of beach nourishment. It includes a sea-level history, maps, diagrams, photos, and a glossary for the scientific terminology. It is provided by the Coastal Services Center of NOAA.

Access this Web site from http://www.myreportlinks.com

Bulldozing the beaches is another method used to strengthen them. Sand is pushed up to make dunes, but this kills creatures living in the upper beach. And it is a form of beach erosion. Each time a beach is replenished with new sand, it destroys plants and animals.

→Beach Armoring

Beach erosion only became a problem when people started to build on the beach. Engineers want to keep the beaches in place to protect the homes and businesses.

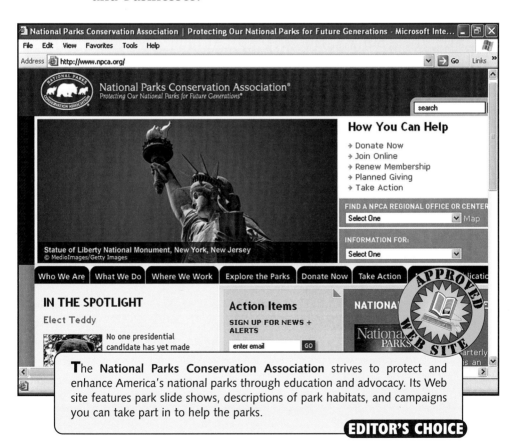

The **National Parks Conservation Association** strives to protect and enhance America's national parks through education and advocacy. Its Web site features park slide shows, descriptions of park habitats, and campaigns you can take part in to help the parks.

EDITOR'S CHOICE

93

In order to fight the ocean and hold it back, seawalls are built along the shore. This is called beach armoring. The walls might be constructed of concrete, wood, rocks, steel, or simple sandbags. Concrete walls line some beaches along Massachusetts, New York, and New Jersey shores. At high tide, there is no beach. Residents can only use the beach at low tide. Studies have shown that once a seawall is built, in twenty-five to fifty years, the beach is completely gone.[4]

Concrete walls may not be built on North Carolina beaches. North Carolina residents may use sandbags as walls to keep the ocean out of their homes. This is a way to make the beaches stronger, and it may help to protect homes and

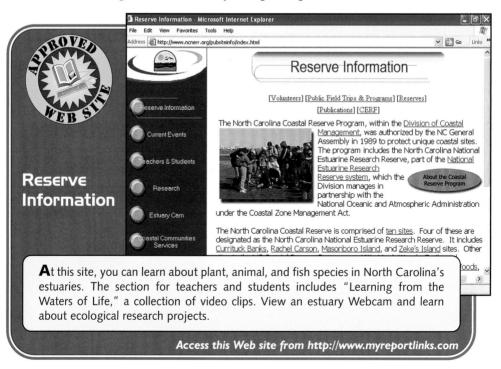

Reserve Information — Microsoft Internet Explorer

File   Edit   View   Favorites   Tools   Help

Address http://www.ncnerr.org/pubsiteinfo/index.html   Go   Links

Reserve Information

[Volunteers] [Public Field Trips & Programs] [Reserves]
[Publications] [CERF]

The North Carolina Coastal Reserve Program, within the Division of Coastal Management, was authorized by the NC General Assembly in 1989 to protect unique coastal sites. The program includes the North Carolina National Estuarine Research Reserve, part of the National Estuarine Research Reserve system, which the Division manages in partnership with the National Oceanic and Atmospheric Administration under the Coastal Zone Management Act.

About the Coastal Reserve Program

The North Carolina Coastal Reserve is comprised of ten sites. Four of these are designated as the North Carolina National Estuarine Research Reserve. It includes Currituck Banks, Rachel Carson, Masonboro Island, and Zeke's Island sites. Other

Reserve Information

Current Events

Teachers & Students

Research

Estuary Cam

Coastal Communities Services

At this site, you can learn about plant, animal, and fish species in North Carolina's estuaries. The section for teachers and students includes "Learning from the Waters of Life," a collection of video clips. View an estuary Webcam and learn about ecological research projects.

Access this Web site from http://www.myreportlinks.com

businesses. But it doesn't generally work. Storms can knock down seawalls whether they are made of concrete or sandbags.

⮕ DEVELOPMENT ON THE RISE

Building homes on the beaches is a new idea. In colonial days, people knew better than to build their homes so close to the ocean. Villages were set far back from the beach, so they were safer. The town of Nags Head was built on the back side of the island away from the beach. But people kept building homes and businesses. Today, the town sits on the edge of the ocean. The sea has moved in too; the sea level has risen and continues to rise.

People love the ocean and spending time near it. Naturally, the demand for more homes along the beach has grown. In the twenty-first century, people have more money to build these homes. A beautiful new beach house by the ocean in the Outer Banks may cost $1 million or more. Of course, the people who own such expensive homes want to protect them. This is where beach armoring plays a role.

Pockets of growth can be seen all along Route 12. Towns like Kill Devil Hills and Nags Head blend into one mass of construction. It's hard to tell where one town ends and the other one starts. Newly built homes line the streets on both sides of

▲ Development, such as these condominiums built right on the beach, is good news for the real estate industry but is doing damage to the Outer Banks.

Route 12. New businesses pop up. More people come to Cape Hatteras National Seashore and the Outer Banks. Congestion, pollution, and development are damaging the Outer Banks.

⊜WHAT TO DO?

The beach, which so many people love, is being destroyed by those who love it! The plan by state and federal agencies is to continue to nourish the beaches of North Carolina. This means that new sand will be brought in. This will help with beach erosion, but it will harm the animals and plants already living there.

There is no doubt that the sea will continue to rise. Global warming is not going to end anytime soon. Glaciers around the world are melting, and sea levels will continue to rise. But homes will still be built along the coastline, and the struggle to protect them and keep the ocean out will also continue. Many people feel there is little they can do about this. Education seems to be the best course of action—teach people about what is happening on the beaches of the Outer Banks, raise their awareness, and hope for change to come.

Chapter
6

A mare and her foal—part of a small band of wild horses—on the beach at Corolla, north of Kitty Hawk on the Outer Banks.

Fun in the Sun

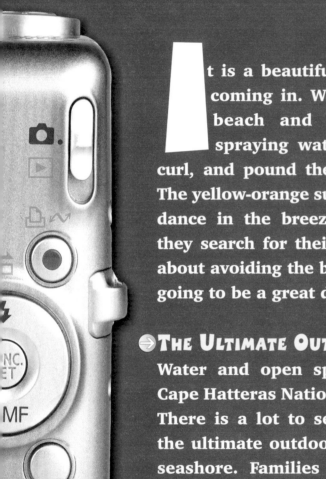

It is a beautiful morning. The tide is coming in. Waves curl up along the beach and slam onto the sand spraying water. The waves retreat, curl, and pound the beach over and over. The yellow-orange sun slowly rises. Sea oats dance in the breeze. Seagulls squawk as they search for their breakfast. Crabs race about avoiding the birds and the waves. It's going to be a great day at the beach!

→ THE ULTIMATE OUTDOOR EXPERIENCE

Water and open space bring families to Cape Hatteras National Seashore each year. There is a lot to see and do. Camping is the ultimate outdoor experience along the seashore. Families can stake their tents right on the beach in designated camping areas at Oregon Inlet, Cape Point, Frisco, and Ocracoke Island.

Camping right on the beach is a unique

experience in itself. There are no trees, and the sun can be very hot. It is important to bring some shade. It can also be very windy. Campers need extra long stakes to tie down their tents securely. Insects are a problem too, so mosquito nets and repellent are a must. Despite these few draw-backs, nothing is better than waking up early and watching the seashore come to life.

⊜A Day at the Beach

My family and I spent some time at Cape Hatteras National Seashore as part of a summer vacation. Our summer cottage was just a few hundred feet from the beach. One day, we set our alarms for 5:30 A.M. It was fun to walk on the beach early in the morning as it came to life. Few people were there. We saw many birds and crabs. The ocean was full of life, and fish swam close to the shore. As we sat on the cool sand and watched the waves roll in, we saw a stingray fly out of the water sev-eral times.

Later in the morning, other people woke up and came to the seashore. The beach started to slowly fill up. People who love to fish walked to the beach. They set up their fishing poles and whipped the lines far out into the water to surf fish. The beach became dotted with fishermen. Cape Point is well known for its big fish and big waves.

Outer Banks of NC, North Carolina's Outer Banks, OBX Vacations, Outer Banks NC Beach Vacation - Microsoft Int...

File   Edit   View   Favorites   Tools   Help

Address   http://www.visitnc.com/where_to_go_coast_obx.asp

explore
north carolina

Home   About NC   Where To Go   What To Do   Where To Stay   Travel Tools   Search   visitnc.com

north carolina coast

Carova
Elizabeth City   Corolla
                        Sanderling
                        Duck
Edenton   Kitty Hawk   Southern Shores
          Albemarle Sound
          Manteo

Plan a visit to Cape Hatteras or many other places in North Carolina. **Visit North Carolina**, the state's official tourism site, discusses where to stay and what to do. Interactive maps and a browsable collection of heritage listings are included.

EDITOR'S CHOICE

A group of kayakers paddled by us as they rowed along the water's edge. They did not come in close; the waves would have tipped them over. They did not paddle too far out either; the water was deep. A motorboat raced by. It was so far out we could not hear it, which was good—it was still quiet on the beach.

As the sun rose higher in the sky, the air became hot. We heard voices coming over the dune as a family of four made its way toward the beach. The family members laid out their towels

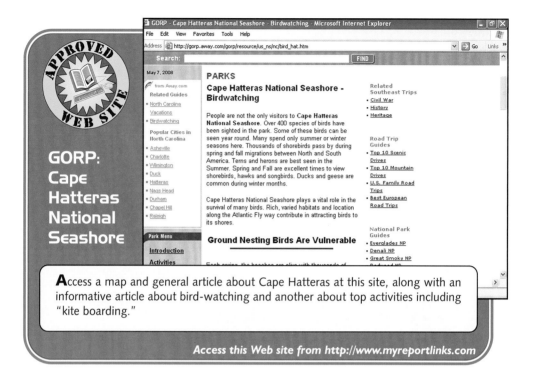

Access a map and general article about Cape Hatteras at this site, along with an informative article about bird-watching and another about top activities including "kite boarding."

Access this Web site from http://www.myreportlinks.com

and blankets and pushed their umbrella firmly in the sand.

The wind had picked up too. The sun was so hot, yet the wind kept the beach comfortable. We watched as children and adults ran into the water. They swam and body surfed. Some of them had boogie boards and caught a wave. We saw other children build sandcastles and decorate them with the many pieces of shells lying about.

We found that swimming in the ocean was not always easy. The waves were rough and, in some places, they were big. Some people have been injured because the waves were so strong. But we were hot and decided to go for a swim.

The difficult part was getting into the water. The waves crashed into us and knocked us down. Once we made it past the waves, swimming became easier. As I stood to get out of the water, a wave knocked me down and dragged me along the beach. I did a somersault in the water and swallowed salt water, which went up my nose. I stood up, gasping for breath, only to be knocked down a second time. When I made it to the warm, soft sand, I had a skinned knee.

Few of the beaches here have lifeguards, so children always need to be supervised. Rip currents are also a danger.

Rip currents are like rivers in the water that flow out to sea. It is frightening to be caught in a

National Weather Service: Rip Current Safety

Rip currents are a phenomenon familiar to residents and visitors at Cape Hatteras. This site sponsored by NOAA's National Weather Service offers safety tips, forecasts, scientific information, and questions and answers on rip currents.

Access this Web site from http://www.myreportlinks.com

rip current. A person's natural instinct is to try to fight it and attempt to swim back to shore. But this effort will only make the person tired and unable to swim. The best thing to do if caught in a rip current is to remain calm. Swim parallel to the shore and then work your way back to shore at an angle.

We saw that some surfers had decided to catch the waves too. Cape Hatteras National Seashore has some of the best waves on the East Coast. Because the Outer Banks are located farther out into the Atlantic Ocean than other coastal areas, there are sandbars and swells. Swells are large waves that come in from the deep sea. There is nothing in the ocean to stop or break up these swells. They can roll in big.

SURFING AND KITE FLYING

Summer is not always the best time to surf, though, unless there is a storm brewing in the tropics. Fall is often the best time to surf. When the weather turns colder, surfers wear wet suits, gloves, and booties to keep warm. Pea Island National Wildlife Refuge, S Turns, Cape Hatteras Lighthouse, Frisco and Ocracoke are just a few of the good places to surf here.

Now the beach swarmed with people, but it was not crowded. There was plenty of space for everyone. Suddenly, the sky became filled with kites. Kite flying is popular on Cape Hatteras National Seashore because there is always a breeze. We dried off, slathered on more sunscreen, and grabbed sandwiches from the cooler. There was more to do at Cape Hatteras National Seashore than swimming and lying in the sun. My family and I decided to explore.

CYCLING

One way to see Cape Hatteras National Seashore is on two wheels. We decided this might be a good way to see the sights, and we rented bikes. Because the main road, Route 12, is parallel to the seashore, it is flat. The National Seashore stretches about seventy-two miles. There is only one hill, and that is the bridge that goes over Oregon Inlet. Still, it is not a difficult hill to ride over.

Two things do make it difficult for the bicyclist: wind and traffic. We noticed that it was harder to pedal our bikes when riding against the wind. It was better to have the wind at our backs to help push us along. Many serious cyclists will plan their day around the wind direction.

Route 12 is a two-lane highway. It's narrow without much room on the sides, and traffic in the summer is very heavy. We soon realized that with cars racing by, it might be a good idea to get off the main road. It was scary to ride a bicycle on the main road with my two children, but the serious bicyclist will enjoy it.

Many people cycle from Bodie Island Lighthouse to Ocracoke Lighthouse in a day. Not only is it a good way to see the sights—such as the three lighthouses—but there are places for cyclists to stop along the way to rest and eat. Also, the forty-minute ferry ride to Ocracoke Island is a nice break.

⊛HIKING

You can expect to do a lot of walking when visiting Cape Hatteras National Seashore, whether it is back and forth to the beach, sightseeing, or hiking. Actually, visitors to the seashore can hike the seventy-two miles along the beach itself. There are many structured trails for hiking, with signs to explain the history or ecosystem of the area. The land is flat, and hiking is easy.

The Bodie Island Dike Trail starts at the Bodie Island Lighthouse. This trail winds through forests and marshes. Benches situated along the way provide good resting points or places to watch the wildlife. The North Pond Wildlife and Salt Flats Wildlife trails are found on Pea Island National Wildlife Refuge.

Buxton Woods Nature Trail, located near Cape Point, takes hikers through a unique ecosystem called the maritime forest. It is the largest maritime forest in North Carolina. It is a cool retreat

▲ Built in 1872, Bodie Light is the third lighthouse constructed on Bodie Island (the first two were destroyed). The light is 156 feet tall and still operates, although visitors cannot enter the lighthouse.

from the hot beaches, but the visitor there can still hear the roar of the ocean just beyond the forest. It is full of wildlife including the dangerous cottonmouth snake, which hikers are warned about.

Ocracoke Island has the Hammock Hills Nature Trail. This trail takes hikers through sand dunes

and a small maritime forest and ends up at a
salt marsh.

→ SIGHTS TO SEE

We decided to check out the famous lighthouses of
the Outer Banks, starting with Bodie Lighthouse.
This lighthouse has an interesting history, which
we read about inside the small museum and visitor center, but we could not climb to the top. It
needs repair.

We then drove south on Route 12 through
small towns like Rodanthe, Waves, and Salvo.
Shops, restaurants, and homes lined the road.
In the cluster of modern-day shops is Chicamacomico Life Saving Station, a historic building and
site located in Rodanthe (see chapter 3). It was
one of the original seven lifesaving stations on the
Outer Banks. Men who worked here saved the
lives of many shipwrecked sailors.

One night, a bonfire was lit on the beach and a
storyteller shared shipwreck and lifesaving stories
around the campfire. It was exciting and a little
creepy!

The most famous lighthouse at Cape Hatteras
National Seashore is Cape Hatteras Light. We
could not wait to learn about the history of this
lighthouse and to climb to the top of it.

We climbed the 268-step-spiral staircase,
which winds around the inside of the lighthouse.

The nonprofit National Parks Foundation helps to maintain and promote America's national parks. On its Web site you can plan a vacation, learn about the Junior Ranger program, and read and submit "inside information" based on park visits.

Access this Web site from http://www.myreportlinks.com

The staircase is narrow, and it was a long, difficult climb. Once we made it to the top, we could not believe what we saw. The view was amazing! The beaches and ocean stretched out for miles. The small town of Hatteras lay below. The sound sat quietly to our northwest. A bird flew by—we too had a bird's-eye view of Cape Hatteras National Seashore.

Back in the car, we drove south again on Route 12. The Frisco Native American Museum and Natural History Center was just ahead. Here, we learned all about the Croatan Indians, their culture, and how they lived on the Outer Banks. A small theater, a gift shop, and guided nature trails are found here.

We stopped at another interesting place called Graveyard of the Atlantic Museum. Here, we learned about maritime history and the many different shipwrecks off the coast.

⇒ FERRY RIDE TO OCRACOKE

In order to get to Ocracoke Island, we had to take a forty-minute ferry ride. We drove our car onto the ferry, and it slowly left the dock once everyone was on board. The wind picked up and seagulls followed our boat. We threw some bread from our lunch to them.

Once we reached Ocracoke Island, we docked and waited our turn to get off the ferry. The island's appearance is much like Hatteras; the National Seashore continues here, and beaches and dunes blanket much of Ocracoke.

Along the road, we saw fences. Stopping at the Pony Pens, we listened to a park ranger introduce some of the ponies still living on the island. They are penned now to keep them safe. These ponies are still considered wild.

Our final destination was the Ocracoke Lighthouse, the second-oldest lighthouse still running in the United States. It is a small lighthouse and is closed to the public, but we walked up to it and took some photos.

We drove around the harbor and stopped at some shops. There are many shops and restaurants in the harbor and a great deal of history. On our way out of the harbor, we made a stop at an ice-cream shop. Ocracoke Island is a fun place to explore.

THE WRIGHT BROTHERS

The visitor to the Outer Banks and Cape Hatteras National Seashore cannot leave without visiting the Wright Brothers National Memorial and Jockey's Ridge. The Wright Brothers are famous for being the first men to fly a powered, heavier-than-air plane. They tested their kites, gliders, and planes at Kitty Hawk, just north of Cape Hatteras National Seashore. The memorial sits on top of Kill Devil Hills, a large sand dune.

Visitors to the park can see the hangars in which the Wright brothers lived and worked, as well as the markers where they first attempted to fly. One museum holds a reproduction of the 1903 flyer and other artifacts are on the site. A national historic landmark, the Wright Brothers National Memorial is fun and educational.

JOCKEY'S RIDGE

Jockey's Ridge State Park is home to the tallest sand dune in the eastern United States. Visitors can slide, roll, and tumble down the dune. My

WILBUR
WRIGHT
ORVILLE
WRIGHT

IN COMMEMORATION OF THE CONQUEST OF THE AIR

▲ *The Wright Brothers National Memorial is located north of Cape Hatteras at Kitty Hawk, N.C. The memorial is on top of Kill Devil Hill, a large sand dune.*

husband and other family members decided to take glider flying lessons. We stood on top of the biggest sand dune and watched. The children rolled down one side of the dune while family members flew off the other side!

Because Jockey's Ridge is a dune, it is always changing. There is a boardwalk, nature trail, gift shop, and picnic area. Visitors are encouraged to wear their shoes because the sand gets very hot.

➔ ROANOKE ISLAND

Although it is not part of Cape Hatteras National Seashore, Roanoke Island is still close enough to visit. The island is located on the Outer Banks between Pamlico Sound and Croatan Sound. The waters surrounding it are calm. Sailing, fishing, and swimming are popular here. And there is a lot to do. Aside from shopping and eating, there is an aquarium, some museums, an art gallery, and an airport.

Roanoke Island also has a rich history. This is where the first settlement (the Lost Colony) was started. Each summer, a play is performed throughout the summer months to educate and entertain people about the Lost Colony.

Festival Park is located on the Manteo waterfront. It brings history to life as children and adults get to see what life was like for American Indians and the early explorers and settlers. There

Jockey's Ridge State Park is the site of the tallest sand dune in the eastern United States. Many people take glider flying lessons there.

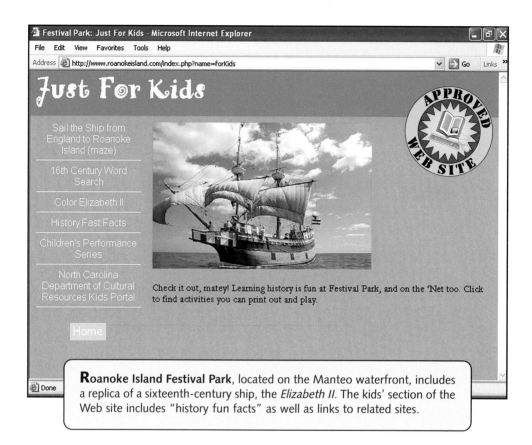

Festival Park: Just For Kids - Microsoft Internet Explorer

File   Edit   View   Favorites   Tools   Help

Address   http://www.roanokeisland.com/index.php?name=forKids

Just For Kids

Sail the Ship from England to Roanoke Island (maze)

16th Century Word Search

Color Elizabeth II

History Fast Facts

Children's Performance Series

North Carolina Department of Cultural Resources Kids Portal

Home

Check it out, matey! Learning history is fun at Festival Park, and on the 'Net too. Click to find activities you can print out and play.

Done

Roanoke Island Festival Park, located on the Manteo waterfront, includes a replica of a sixteenth-century ship, the *Elizabeth II*. The kids' section of the Web site includes "history fun facts" as well as links to related sites.

is a reproduction of a sixteenth-century ship named *Elizabeth II*. It was built like the original ship that brought the first settlers in 1585.

⊖ REST AND RELAXATION

With all there is to do at Cape Hatteras National Seashore and surrounding areas, it can be tiring. We were happy to return to our cottage. Sometimes, the best thing to do at the seashore is just rest and relax. Swaying in a hammock and feeling the breeze gently sweep our faces, we read books and watched the sunset.

At Cape Hatteras National Seashore, the sunset is as beautiful as the sunrise. As the orange ball drifts to the horizon, promising another hot beach day to come, people head home. The beach quiets. One by one, stars twinkle in the dark sky.

It was another clear night. We headed down to the beach. The children went to the water's edge. The water was glowing. Blue-green lights glowed in the sand where the waves just crashed. We stomped on the sand to make the lights appear.

These lights are actually tiny single-celled algae. Their glow, called bioluminescence, is actually a defense mechanism to scare off predators. It happens when the algae are shaken or stirred. These creatures are similar to fireflies because they both create light through a chemical reaction.

While the children stomped on the sand at the edge of the ocean and squealed with laughter, the adults made a fire pit. Sand was cleared away for the pit to be made. We lay on blankets and watched the shooting stars and satellites overhead. We passed potato chips and shared stories. Bonfires lit up the beaches and dotted the shoreline. There is so much for families to enjoy from sunrise to sunset at the beach known as Cape Hatteras National Seashore.

Report Links

▶**Cape Hatteras National Seashore**
Editor's Choice Learn all about Cape Hatteras, and plan a visit!

▶**National Parks Conservation Association**
Editor's Choice Read about the natural resources in our national parks, and conservation efforts.

▶**Outer Banks of North Carolina**
Editor's Choice Discover more about the barrier islands that form the Outer Banks.

▶**Visit North Carolina**
Editor's Choice Explore the regions and history of North Carolina, and plan a trip there.

▶**Geology Fieldnotes: Cape Hatteras National Seashore, North Carolina**
Editor's Choice Learn about the geology of Cape Hatteras National Seashore.

▶**Great Lighthouses: Lighthouses of the South Atlantic**
Editor's Choice Read about historical lighthouses on the Atlantic coast.

▶**Blackbeard the Pirate**
Read about the most famous pirate of all, Blackbeard, and his ship, *Queen Anne's Revenge.*

▶**Civilian Conservation Corps Alumni**
Learn about the people who built sand dunes in the 1930s that are still protecting Cape Hatteras.

▶**First English Settlement in the New World**
Read about the Europeans who first explored the coast of modern-day North Carolina.

▶**Fort Raleigh National Historic Site**
Learn about the first English settlement in what would become North Carolina.

▶**Frisco Native American Museum and Natural History Center**
Learn much more about American Indian culture at the Web site of this museum in Hatteras, N.C.

▶**Geologic Regimes of the Atlantic and Gulf Coasts**
Beach nourishment is a controversial practice. At this site, you can read arguments for and against it.

▶**Geologic Time—The Story of a Changing Earth**
Get an understanding of the different eras of time and the changes they have brought to the earth.

▶**GORP: Cape Hatteras National Seashore**
Learn more about Cape Hatteras through the articles on this site.

▶**Graveyard of the Atlantic Museum**
Read about efforts to recover artifacts from shipwrecks, and the maritime battles that caused them.

Report Links

The Internet sites described below can be accessed at
http://www.myreportlinks.com

▶**Historical Highlights of North Carolina**
Learn the history of North Carolina from early American Indian life to the present.

▶**History and Lore of Blackbeard the Pyrate**
Learn more about the notorious pirate Blackbeard and his castle.

▶**Institute of Nautical Archaeology**
Find out how researchers explore shipwrecks, and what they have found.

▶**The Mariners' Museum**
See history come alive with a 3-D video reenactment of the sinking of the USS *Monitor*.

▶**National Hurricane Survival Initiative**
Learn about the threat posed by hurricanes and what you can do to be prepared.

▶**National Parks Foundation**
Find out how the foundation aims to strengthen the connection between Americans and their parks.

▶**National Underwater and Marine Agency**
Learn about efforts to salvage artifacts from shipwrecks.

▶**National Weather Service: Rip Current Safety**
Find out what rip currents are, what effects they have, and how you can avoid them.

▶**Native American Indian Genealogy**
Explore a wealth of information about American Indian history and genealogy.

▶**N.C. Wildlife Resources Commission: Fishing**
Learn when and where you can fish at Cape Hatteras and throughout North Carolina.

▶**Pea Island National Wildlife Refuge**
Discover Pea Island, where bird-watchers can observe more than four hundred species!

▶**Reserve Information**
Get to know about North Carolina's coastal reserve program.

▶**Roanoke Island Festival Park**
Explore the history, arts, and culture of Roanoke Island.

▶**Sand Dunes**
Learn about the science behind sand dunes and the role they play.

▶**Tales From the Deep**
Read about the search for pirate ships and about the pirates who sailed them.

barrier islands—Islands that are formed between the ocean and the mainland.

beach armoring—When seawalls and jetties are built to protect homes and businesses from the ocean.

beach nourishment—The process of bringing new sand in from other places to replace sand that has been eroded or washed away.

beach ridge—A wave-swept ridge that runs parallel to a shoreline.

bioluminescence—When a living organism makes light.

continental shelf—Part of the continent that is under the sea.

daymark—The identification used on lighthouses. Bodie Light has black-and-white stripes. Cape Hatteras Light has black-and-white-spiral stripes, and Ocracoke Light is all white.

dunes—A land feature formed from the buildup of windblown sand. It may be bare or have plants.

endangered—Something that is threatened.

erosion—The loss of sand from a beach that wears away the shoreline.

fossils—A trace of an organism from a past geological age.

global warming—A gradual warming of the earth's atmosphere created by burning fossil fuels and pollutants.

habitat—The place where a plant or animal lives.

Ice Age—Period that ended an estimated ten thousand years ago, when much of the North American continent was covered in ice. Also called the glacial period.

mariners—Men and women who sail on ships and boats.

maritime forest—A forest that borders on the sea.

migration—When birds move from place to place, often in the fall, to reach warmer habitats.

piracy—The act of being a pirate, or one who robs at sea.

plunder—To take goods by force.

ridgeline—A long narrow chain of hills and mountains.

sediment—Mineral or organic material left by water, air, or ice.

shell hash—Broken shells on a beach.

sound—A narrow body of water between an island and the mainland.

swash—The final remains of a wave as it rolls up on the beach.

Chapter 1. Shiver Me Timbers!

1. St. Thomas History and Pirate Lore, "Blackbeard the Pirate," 2000–2006, <http://www.blackbeardscastle.com/st-thomas-history.htm> (October 6, 2006).

2. Outer Banks Chamber of Commerce, "A Brief History of Ocracoke," 2007, <http://www.outerbankschamber.com/relocation/history/ocracoke.cfm> (October 29, 2007).

Chapter 2. The Ever-Changing Seashore

1. Ralph C. Heath, "Origins of the Hatteras Island," *The Best of the Hatteras Monitor,* Vol. 1, 1999, p. 2.

2. Ibid.

3. Discoverers Web. "Giovanni da Verrazzano," n.d., <http://www.win.tue.nl/~engels/discovery/verrazzano.html> (November 17, 2006).

4. "Driving Along," *The Best of the Hatteras Monitor,* Vol. 1, 1999, p. 1.

5. Ibid.

6. Charles E. Cobb, Jr., "Awash in Change," *National Geographic,* October 1987, vol. 172, no. 4, p. 511.

7. David Stapleton, *Famous Pirates,* n.d., <http://www.kipar.org/piratical-resources/pirate-fame.html#R> (April 1, 2007).

8. Outer Beaches Realty, Inc., "Outer Banks History," 1997–2006, <http://www.outerbeaches.com/OuterBanksHistory> (November 21, 2006).

Chapter 3. Part Land, Part Sea

1. Department of the Navy, Naval Historical Center, "*USS Merrimack,*" (May 3, 2001) <http://www.history.navy.mil/photos/sh-usn/usnsh-m/merimak2.htm> (November 15, 2007).

2. David Stick, *Graveyard of the Atlantic* (Chapel Hill, N.C.: The University of North Carolina Press, 1975), p. 54.

3. Department of the Navy, Naval Historical Center, *"USS Merrimack."*

4. "1861 to the Present: An Interactive Story of the Monitor," *The USS Monitor Center,* 2005, <http://www.monitorcenter.org/> (November 25, 2006).

5. Stick, p. 229.

6. Douglas Bingham, U.S. Coast Guard Lightship Sailors, "Lightships of Diamond Shoals," (2003), <http://www.uscglightshipsailors.org/lightships_of_diamond_shoals_017.htm> (November 15, 2006).

7. Outer Banks Chamber of Commerce, "Cape Hatteras Lighthouse," (2003), <http://www.outerbankschamber.com/relocation/history/capehatteras.cfm>

Chapter 4. Bubble Holes and Barking Sand

1. Molly P. Harrison, *Exploring Cape Hatteras and Cape Lookout National Seashore* (Guilford, Conn.: Falcon, 2003), p. xxi.

2. Orrin H. Pilkey, Tracy M. Rice, and William J. Neal, *How to Read a North Carolina Beach* (Chapel Hill, N.C.: The University of North Carolina Press, 2004), p. 104.

3. David L. Nash, Sea Oats Research, *Education and Production,* March 24, 2003, <http://www.cals.ncsu.edu/specialty_crops/publications/reports/nash.html> (October 28, 2006).

4. Harrison, p. 36.

5. Ibid., p. xviii.

Chapter 5. Extreme Impact

1. "Hurricanes," *The Best of the Hatteras Monitor,* vol. 1, 1999, p. 14.

2. "When Will a Category Five Hurricane Strike the Outer Banks?," September 14, 2005, <http://www.sprol.com/?p=259> (November 28, 2006).

3. Ibid.

4. Orrin H. Pilkey, Tracy Monegan Rice, and William J. Neal. *How to Read a North Carolina Beach* (Chapel Hill, N.C.: The University of North Carolina Press, 2004), p. 134.

Burgan, Michael. *Battle of the Ironclads.* Minneapolis: Compass Point Books, 2006.

Fritz, Jean. *The Lost Colony of Roanoke.* New York: Putnam Juvenile, 2004.

Harrison, Molly Perkins. *It Happened on the Outer Banks.* Guilford, Conn.: Globe Pequot, 2005.

Matthews, John. *Pirates.* New York: Atheneum, 2006.

O'Brian, Patrick. *Duel of the Ironclads: The Monitor vs. the Virginia.* New York: Walker & Co., 2003.

Platt, Richard. *Shipwreck.* New York: DK Publishing, 2005.

Press, Petra. *The Cherokee.* Minneapolis: Compass Point Books, 2002.

Rafle, Sarah. *North Carolina, the Tar Heel State.* Milwaukee: World Almanac Library, 2002.

Reed, Jennifer. *Wilbur and Orville Wright.* Berkeley Heights, N.J.: MyReportLinks.com Books, 2008.

Weatherford, Carole Boston. *Sink or Swim: African-American Lifesavers of the Outer Banks.* Wilmington, N.C.: Coastal Carolina Press, 1999.